The Developme
Intelligence

How do children learn about the expression and meaning of emotions – both happy and sad? This book answers questions regarding the foundation of emotional intelligence, and examines how children become emotionally literate as they are socialized into their family environment from birth to 2 years of age. These early stages are vitally important in teaching children to understand themselves and others, as well as how to relate to people, and how to adapt to and cope with their immediate surroundings.

In order to examine the development of emotional intelligence, the author presents an overview of the literature on the subject and in the second part of the book presents a case study in which the concepts introduced in the first part of the book are revisited. Based on daily tape-recorded 'conversations' between a baby and her father, the data demonstrate how, over a two-year period, the child learns to express and understand emotions within social interactions. This capacity to reason with emotions is examined through four areas: perceiving emotion, integrating emotion, understanding emotion and managing emotion.

The Development of Emotional Intelligence adds a new perspective to the theoretical debate on emotions and how they develop. It will be of great interest to psychologists and any professionals dealing with families. It will also be helpful reading for parents.

Nadja Reissland is a Senior Lecturer in the Department of Psychology at Durham University. Her research concerns emotional development from the prenatal period to early childhood in relation to maternal stress and depression. Her latest research examines fetal facial expressions in utero.

Concepts in Developmental Psychology
Series editor: David Cohen

The Development of Emotional Intelligence

A Case Study

Nadja Reissland

Routledge
Taylor & Francis Group

LONDON AND NEW YORK

First published 2012
by Routledge
27 Church Road, Hove, East Sussex BN3 2FA

Simultaneously published in the USA and Canada
by Routledge
711 Third Avenue, New York NY 10017

*Routledge is an imprint of the Taylor & Francis Group, an informa
business*

British Library Cataloguing in Publication Data
A catalogue record for this book is available from the British Library

Library of Congress Cataloging-in-Publication Data
Reissland, Nadja.
　The development of emotional intelligence : a case study / Nadja
Reissland.
　　p. cm. – (Concepts in developmental psychology)
　Includes bibliographical references and index.
　ISBN 978-0-415-35951-1 (hbk.) – ISBN 978-0-415-35952-8 (pbk.)
1. Emotional intelligence. 2. Emotions in children. 3. Child
psychology. I. Title.
　BF576.R45 2012
　155.42'224–dc23

　　　　　　　　　　　　　　　　　　　　　　　　　　　2011043704

ISBN: 978-0-415-35951-1 (hbk)
ISBN: 978-0-415-35952-8 (pbk)
ISBN: 978-0-203-00749-5 (ebk)

Typeset in Times by Garfield Morgan, Swansea, West Glamorgan
Cover design by Lisa Dynan

Printed by Bell & Bain Ltd., Glasgow

Dedicated to Toto and Christopher

In memory of Richard

Contents

Foreword

When I was 12 years old a nun told me to hug a dead animal so as to feel closer to my father. Although I was a little puzzled by the prospect of 'finding' my father in whatever roadkill or unfortunate bird I happened to come across, it did sound more appealing than just 'praying for his soul', which was the suggestion offered by my class teacher. I therefore, somewhat gleefully, relayed the advice back to my mother. Naturally she was horrified and absolutely forbade *any* ritualistic interactions with animals on the spot.

In retrospect, it was a ridiculous proposal and it does seem incredible it was even a suggestion; however, I have grown to understand why well-intentioned people feel the need to offer such misguided advice. To put it bluntly, death is socially awkward. No one knows how to respond. The desire to express one's sympathy is balanced with the more fervent desire not to say the wrong thing. Not to diminish the death, but not to overplay it either.

If discussing the death of a parent is difficult with an adult, it is even more so when talking with a child about the death of their parent. This is especially true in cases where it is the father who died when the child was relatively young.

It is easy to dismiss the impact a father can have in the early months of his daughter's life. Common perceptions seem to be that it is the mother who has the 'special bond' with the baby and that the father only comes to the fore once the daughter can walk, talk and needs to be taught how to climb a tree, protected from adolescent boyfriends or when she needs money.

This book challenges this presumption. It demonstrates that the father's bond with his daughter can be as strong and as fundamental as the mother's. That simply by taking the time to listen to his daughter and communicate with her, even when she is just at the babbling stage, the father can shape the development of her emotions and later, the language she will use to describe these emotions. This is a service that cannot be dismissed lightly. As the case study in the second part of the book demonstrates, my ability to effectively communicate my feelings, to explore new emotions and learn their meanings was tested once my father died.

I have just one particularly vivid memory of the aftermath of my father's death. My father used to make popcorn for me in a large blue casserole pan. He would place the popcorn kernels in the pan, cover it with its heavy lid and heat it slowly. After a few minutes we would start to hear the dull thump of the popping corn hitting the lid. As the thuds became more insistent, my father would lift the lid off the pan and we would watch the popcorn zinging all over the kitchen. Admittedly this was a fairly idiosyncratic way of making popcorn (there was rarely any popcorn left by the end), but I remember it being fun.

Some time after my father died, I went to a friend's house and her father suggested that we make popcorn as a treat. I watched as he imitated my father's method of putting the kernels in the pan and heating it. However, he did not react to those first popping sounds by lifting the lid.

As the sound grew more frenzied I became concerned that we were missing the best bit of making popcorn. In a matter of minutes the popping stopped, then died away. Her father turned to us: 'There. Wasn't that exciting?' It wasn't. It was at this moment that I realized that this was something only *my* father had done and that now that he was dead, I would never have popcorn made for me in the same way again.

A small thing, I know, but it is the only distinct memory I have of my grief following my father's death. I had always assumed that I was too young to understand death and therefore also too young to grieve. This book showed me otherwise. It made me remember that no one can truly say that they understand death, they can only accept it.

A child's acceptance of a situation is naturally very different to an adult's acceptance. And maybe a child's acceptance of a life-altering event, like death, can be described as being more fluid than that of an adult.

The sheer number of books about death – how to cope with death, grieving – all indicate that adults feel uncomfortable, not only with not understanding such a fundamental part of life but also with their inability to control or predict their response to it. They want to read, to learn, to match their emotions to the prescribed twelve steps of grief or ten steps of healing, to ensure that their response is 'normal' and that they spend the appropriate amount of time 'getting over it'. It seems to me that this places an unnecessary strain on a person already coping with great emotional upheaval.

A child is not aware of the 'normal' or 'traditional' way to mourn a death and has only their own way. I'm not suggesting that a child's way is any better; however, their response is more likely to be spontaneous and unconstrained by societal or personal expectations. They can ask whatever questions cross their mind, without worrying about looking foolish, and can react with whatever emotion comes to them at a given time.

The depiction of my response in the aftermath of my father's death indicates that even if a child does not talk about 'getting over' or 'moving on' from a loss, it finds other ways of expressing that this process is happening (in my case through the drawings of families in houses).

Consequently, as well as studying the development of emotional intelligence in a child and a portrayal of a father's relationship with his daughter, this book also offers an understanding of how children cope with bereavement. It describes how parents can begin to establish emotionally intelligent habits in their children that will help them as they confront life, and everything that it will throw at them.

Toto

Acknowledgements

Chapter 7: 'The language of emotions from the first months of life', from Reissland, N. (2006) Teaching a baby the language of emotions: A father's experience. *Zero-To-Three*, 27: 42–48.

Chapter 8: 'Acoustic aspects of emotion talk', from Reissland, N. (1998) The pitch of 'real' and 'rhetorical' questions directed by a father to his daughter: A longitudinal case study. *Infant Behavior and Development*, 21 (4): 793–798.

Chapter 12: 'Toto's experience of her father's death', from Reissland, N. (1995) How angels become real. *Common Knowledge*, 4: 1–6.

Part I

Overview of the literature on emotional intelligence

1 Introduction

Overview

Emotional intelligence (EI) has been taught for a very long time: 'Since the beginning of civilization, parents and teachers have been helping children to better understand and control their emotions and those of others' (Cherniss 2004: 319). Emotional intelligence helps to predict success in social situations because it reflects how a person applies knowledge to the immediate situation. Hence, if one wants to measure EI, one should measure the degree of common sense. Bar-On (1997) defined emotional intelligence as: 'an array of personal, emotional, and social competencies and skills that influence one's ability to succeed in coping with environmental demands and pressures'. EI is therefore an important factor in determining one's ability to succeed in life and directly influence one's general psychological well-being in terms of overall emotional health. This construct implies that people have different abilities to perceive, understand and manage emotions.

Judging by the many websites which offer to teach emotional intelligence, the topic is seen as being vital to human development. Given the emphasis placed on emotional intelligence together with research indicating that emotional development starts from birth, there is an urgent need to examine not only emotional development in general but also the development of one aspect of emotional development, namely the growth of emotional intelligence in the context of child development.

This book addresses some of the questions on the first steps taken in helping a baby becoming a person able to apply emotional intelligence in the day-to-day context. With this book, the reader will get an insight into how emotions are socialized in context and how emotional intelligence might grow in the context of a father's interactions with his daughter. Additionally, the role of a father, which has been less extensively studied (e.g. Pruett 1998) than the role of the mother in development generally and in emotional development particularly, will be discussed.

This book brings together two different types of inquiry: an academic overview of the topic of emotional intelligence in various contexts and a case study of one baby's development. The academic overview and the case study are reported in two parts of the book. The first part concerns emotional intelligence in terms of theories and published research mostly in refereed journals and to a lesser extent in books written by experts. The second part is about one child's journey on the road to becoming emotionally intelligent, reported through the eyes of her father. This part of the book is based on transcripts of tape-recordings, in which the father recounts his daughter's behaviour. The audiotapes are recorded by the father while he engages with his daughter, for example, while changing her nappy, dressing her, feeding her and playing with her from the time the baby is 1 month old to the time when she has reached 4 years of age and her father is dying of cancer. Given that all records are audiotapes, the baby's development is mainly reflected through the voice of her father and to a lesser extent through her vocalizations, with no direct observation of the child's behaviours.

Background to the study of emotional intelligence

Research on the topic of emotional intelligence relates to questions of how people perceive, control and evaluate emotions. However, there is still extensive discussion on definitions of emotional intelligence, whether it is a valid concept and how it relates to cognition and social performance (Mayer et al. 2008). Various definitions of EI and the question of whether or not the EI construct is helpful in understanding development are topics addressed in Chapter 1. One aspect of EI that people at least in western society seem to agree on is that emotional development is essential for healthy psychological functioning. In order to show emotions in appropriate contexts, which is part of emotionally intelligent functioning, children need to be able to 'read' the emotions of others both in terms of being able to identify facial expressions and labelling emotions as well as listening to the pitch of voice in which the emotion is expressed. These developments will be discussed in more detail in Chapter 2. A number of studies have shown that healthy psychological functioning which is facilitated by emotional intelligence as well as psychological dysfunction, are closely related to health in general. For example, negative emotions lower the immune system of a person and lead to an increased risk of disease. In relation to children it has been linked to specific areas of functioning such as school performance. The topic of health will be discussed in Chapter 6.

EI in the context of emotional development

In spite of the interest in the topic of emotional intelligence, the question of how an infant becomes an emotionally competent adult is still not clear. Although we do know that the influence of parents, as socialization agents, is crucial to infant development of emotion understanding and expression (Saarni 1999), the process of development needs still to be clarified. It is agreed that communication about emotions and social-emotional development begins at birth (Cohen 2003). A child's learning about emotions has been studied in the context of parental socialization of children's emotions. For example, Gottman and Declaire (1997) describe how a 2 year old's temper tantrum for her toy zebra is channelled into sleep by her father's empathetic understanding of her frustration. This topic in relation to the growth of emotional intelligence is explored in Chapter 3, where the language of emotional intelligence is discussed.

Novel approach to studying the development of EI

The novel approach of this book is that, rather than analysing the child's behaviour directly, the father is used as a mirror in which we can observe the child's behaviour. Hence, I analyse language used by the father in order to identify how changes in adult language relate to the child's growing understanding of that language. It is the father's interpretations of his daughter's understanding which are used in this context. One might argue that the child does not understand anything at this early age. However, one might also argue that 'understanding' entails changes in behaviour based on pitch variations in speech and this is the level of understanding which I refer to in this book. Although clearly a 9-month-old baby does not have the vocabulary to understand her father's sophisticated speech, still the baby reacts to what the father says and this reaction is reflected in her father's comments on those reactions. Emotion words have been analysed extensively; less is known about the words which we use to describe emotions evoked by the melody of language. Words spoken with different intonation will evoke different understanding of those words such that asking a child to come and look can be said in a loving way or with surprise or anger for example. A young baby, who does not understand the vocabulary, will still understand the meaning of an utterance. Research has shown that in fact adults will disregard the actual words spoken at times. For example, responding to a greeting with 'I am well' will be interpreted as truthful or just polite depending on the intonation of the response. This leads to the surprising finding that babies, not knowing any words, and adults, knowing that the same word can have different meanings, rely more on the melody of language to derive meaning than 5 year olds, who are starting to become proficient in language, and who rely on the spoken words to understand the meaning of these words.

Emotional discourse and EI

Emotional discourse is an important aspect of emotional development in general and the development of emotional intelligence in particular. According to Zeidner et al. (2003), early language-dependent skill learning is governed by reinforcement and modelling processes. In simplified terms, reinforcement helps the child to learn what is good or bad by getting praised or scolded. Modelling desirable behaviours means the child can imitate actions observed and behave accordingly. Subsequent insightful learning is influenced by emotional discourse with parents and others. Even though emotions are seen to be important their function in development has been neglected: 'Although emotion is considered to be a corner stone of human experience many current theoretical models and the research bodies they have generated have not adequately considered the role of emotion in development and psychopathology' (Southam-Gerow and Kendall 2002: 189–190). The latest interest in emotion has been fuelled by the concepts, among others, of emotional intelligence, emotional competence and emotional education in a variety of educational, scientific, medical and legislative domains (e.g. Buck 1993; Goleman 1995; Greenberg et al. 1995; Salovey and Sluyter 1997).

Emotion socialization and EI

Emotion socialization occurs both through direct instruction and contingent responding as well as modelling and social referencing. A parent might tell the baby not to throw food from the high chair, or might smile when trying to elicit a smile from a baby or instruct the baby to say 'thank you' when receiving a gift. Infants often glance at their mother or father when they are uncertain of the situation and want to know whether it is, for example, safe to touch an unfamiliar toy. How to understand other people's emotions is related to an empathetic ability which allows people to 'feel' what other people might be feeling. This topic is discussed in Chapter 5 as well as in the case study. It has long been acknowledged that the melody of language teaches the baby about how to interpret daily events. For example, a mother will express her surprise in a higher pitch when the baby does not show surprise during play than when the baby has learned that the situation is surprising (Reissland et al. 2002). Mothers will talk in a higher pitch when they interact with their baby in a play situation than in an ordinary situation (Reissland and Snow 1996) and they will express information with varying pitch depending on whether they teach their infant about positive or negative events in the environment (e.g. Fernald 1992). One important part of the socialization of emotional functioning concerns the ability to regulate emotions, which is the topic of Chapter 4.

The case study

In spite of the fact that there is interest in emotional development in general and emotional intelligence in particular, very little research has been carried out concerning the beginnings of emotion as it develops into intelligent emotional functioning in a social context. This is the topic of the second part of this book. What does it mean for a child to become emotionally intelligent? How does a baby learn about emotions in the context of parent–child interaction from birth to 2 years of age? In order to examine this question the social context of first use of emotion words by the father and the development and change over a two-year period are examined from both the baby's and the parent's point of view. The data are based on daily tape-recorded 'conversations' between a baby daughter and her father. This case study shows clearly via the observations recorded by the father how over a two-year period a child learns to express and understand emotions in social interaction. This capacity to reason with emotion will be examined in four areas: to perceive emotion, to integrate it, to understand it and to manage it.

The importance of the father and EI

The importance of a father's influence on his child's emotional development should not be underestimated. In a study on fathers' influence on their children's cognitive and emotional development in toddlers, Cabrera et al. (2007) argued that what was termed a father's 'supportiveness' was positively associated with children's emotional regulation at 2 years of age and in pre-school. In contrast, fathers who were deemed to be intrusive had a negative effect on their infants' emotional development. Intrusiveness was negatively related to emotional functioning in terms of the ability to regulate their emotions when the child had reached 2 years of age.

The idea that different cultures manage emotions differently has been demonstrated eloquently in a book by Daniel Everett (2008), which discusses the Pirahã people, who seem to live in the present and who could be conceived of in western culture as heartless or cruel, but who according to Everett have just a different world view which serves them well in their society and their environment. Emotional intelligence is tactical, in that it relates to immediate demands of a situation, while cognitive intelligence is strategic, in that it relates to long term goals or abilities to plan for the future. In that sense the Pirahã, who according to Everett (2008) live more or less exclusively in the present with little regard for past or future, should show a high degree of emotional intelligence.

EI in infancy

Although the concept of emotional intelligence has been extensively used in the context of adult education, helping to train high-level executives, emotional development begins from birth. However, there is a gap, in terms of the age at which emotional intelligence has been tested. Most research is concerned with adults, although the most recent addition to the EI inventory tests children as young as 7 years of age. Still, apart from Saarni (1999), very few studies have linked emotional competence to children below the age of 7 years and to my knowledge no one has looked comprehensively at the foundations of emotional intelligence from birth. This is reflected in some of the definitions of emotional intelligence, such as Mayer et al. (2008: 527), who state that: 'Emotional Intelligence (EI) is the ability to carry out accurate reasoning focused on emotions and the ability to use emotions and emotional knowledge to enhance thought', which cannot be tested at this very young age when the child does not yet have language or is barely able to speak. Nevertheless, the foundations for emotionally intelligent functioning are set in infancy and the question of what happens in very early development is the question which the second part of this book addresses.

The second part of this book examines, with the help of audio-diary data of a case study, the foundations of emotional intelligence in terms of the development of understanding and expression of emotion. The main question addressed in the second part of this book examines emotional development, specifically the development of emotionally intelligent functioning in a social context. According to Bar-On (1997), emotional intelligence is concerned with understanding oneself and others, relating to people, and adapting to and coping with the immediate surroundings, which increases a person's ability to be more successful in dealing with environmental demands. Specifically, the case study presented in this book examines the context in which a baby and her father learn about emotions by studying the development of emotional functioning as it unfolds while an American father, a Professor of Anthropology, who spoke various languages, and had lived in many countries of the world, interacts with his daughter, who was brought up in the UK and Germany. Their development is mainly examined in the first two years of life through audio recordings made by the father, apart from Chapter 12, which deals with what is arguably the most difficult situation we have to cope with, namely the death of a loved one. Toto's father died of brain cancer. The experience of his last few months of life and eventual death at home is recounted through the eyes of his daughter.

Labelling emotions in the context of EI growth

Given the intrinsic link, at least in western cultures, of emotional development and communication about emotions, Chapter 7 illustrates through the father's comments on his daughter's behaviours the emotional development of the child from 1 month of age to the time when the baby is at the two word stage. We observe development by examining the father's emotional labels attributed to his daughter's behaviour by analysing the frequency and context in which he uses the emotional labels of happiness, sadness, anger and fear.

One aspect of emotionally intelligent behaviour is the ability to think about emotions. Hence, Chapter 7 examines how the father makes his daughter aware of differences between thinking and feeling. This chapter concentrates on types of questions asked in the context of emotionally charged situations and analysed questions asking about the child's emotions (e.g. What do you feel?) and compared them to questions asking about the child's thoughts (e.g. What do you think?). Furthermore, the child's developing ability to perceive emotional messages, again through the eyes of the father, which are carried in sound rather than the words of the message, are discussed in Chapter 8. Specifically, given that pitch carries the meaning of the message, and that different types of questions carry different meanings (Snow 1977), parents differentiate types of questions with differing pitch of voice. They distinguish in their pitch of voice between questions which require the child to take her turn in the conversation and questions which do not require an answer nor give leave for the child to speak.

Chapter 9 looks in more detail at how father and baby communicate by examining regularly recurring routines or frames, which are defined as either rigid and unchanging or creative and changing behavioural interactions. Fogel et al. (2002) analysed these frames in a case study of one child and her mother's behavioural interactions during three periods, namely, 0–6 months, 6–12 months and 12–18 months. The mutual influence of father and infant is analysed in this book by studying verbal rather than behavioural frames. Basic to development in general and emotional development in particular is the child's ability to distinguish the self 'I' from the other 'You', as it allows the child to make sense of his or her emotions vis-à-vis the other's emotions. Hence the development of emotional intelligent behaviour in the baby is observed in two aspects of interaction: the changing use of personal pronouns in the father's speech as he perceives her developing abilities and the child's changing behaviour, recorded by the father, in relation to his emotional reactions.

Teasing and EI

One of the special features that fathers in contrast to most mothers show, namely their propensity to engage in verbal and nonverbal teasing with their children (Gleason 1975; Hopper et al. 1983; Pecheux and Labrell 1994; Reissland 1998), is the topic of Chapter 10. Teasing can elicit a positive bond with the person, reflecting an intimate bond in a relationship (Eder 1991; Sharkey 1992), or it may be hostile (Warm 1997). In Chapter 10, EI is examined in relation to teasing behaviour and how it changes in context and style. The father teases his daughter from the first recorded interactions. Teasing varies by topic, such as his daughter's sleep patterns, how she walks and how she talks. As his daughter matures, she starts teasing her father in her turn and thereby shows her growing emotional understanding by being able to laugh about her own behaviours and manipulate her father's emotions.

EI and cognitive development

Chapter 11 concerns research on emotional development in relation to cognitive development in infancy (Sroufe and Wunsch 1972). Given that emotional intelligence plays an important role in determining a person's ability to succeed in life and directly influences a person's psychological well-being in terms of their emotional health, explanations of emotional experiences might indeed foster children's understanding of the breadth of a specific emotion, such as happiness, delight, elation or contentment. In the first year of life, positive emotional expression is a developmental process, which progresses from smile to laughter. Especially at the younger age the infant does not laugh but seems to smile and her father labels these smiles. Later she is able to express laughter which can be heard on the audiotapes. According to Tracy and Robins (2008), emotion recognition is automatic and requires only minimal cognitive resources. However, even if adults can recognize emotions subliminally (Winkielman et al. 2005), there needs to be some developmental process, which allows the social construction of these emotions in specific contexts. The present study demonstrates that emotional expression of the child changes over time, as commented on by the father. The father labels these emotions for her and links them to what he perceives as appropriate social situations. Hence, by labelling the situations, which make her laugh, she learns about events that make her happy. Even though, events which make the father and his daughter happy differ. This is indicated by the fact that in the context of father–daughter interactions, father and daughter express laughter in relation to different aspects of the situation. In spite of the fact that father and daughter laugh at different aspects of the situation, they are joined in laughter in the same context, which makes their laughter a social event.

EI and death

The topic of Chapter 12 is how young children cope with the ultimate loss, namely death, and its relation to emotional intelligence. This chapter recounts how the child deals with the illness and impending death of her father and hence gives an insight into how her father's teaching of emotions might have contributed to her way of coping with his death. This chapter is based on a diary kept by her mother as well as drawings by Toto. According to Kübler-Ross (1969), one can discern a 'grief cycle' representing how people cope with death. This cycle is evident not only for the person dying but also for the people affected by the death. Initial paralysis at hearing the bad news results in shock, which is followed by denial. Often people become angry and then they try to bargain. After the realization that bargaining is futile, depression sets in. This might be followed by a stage in which the person looks for realistic solutions to the problem and the final stage is the acceptance stage in which the person accepts what is happening and moves forward.

This book is a journey in which we follow one child's development over time. It emphasizes the role Toto's father played in her early life. She has developed into a young woman who carries the enduring teachings of her father within her and into the world.

2 Emotional intelligence

Models and controversies

Ever since Goleman (1995) had a bestseller with his book on emotional intelligence, research has focused on whether or not people who are emotionally intelligent have an advantage in society and life in general. Before Goleman's popularization of emotional intelligence, there were other researchers such as Gardner (1983), who argued that intelligence needed not only a cognitive but also an emotional component, which helped people to excel in social interactions. Although much has been written about emotional intelligence in adults, there are few publications dealing specifically with the development of emotional intelligence in infancy. The second part of the book will deal with this specific question in various domains with the help of one baby's development of her emotional intelligence, which is charted over time.

The first part of the book relates to what has been discovered so far in terms of the nature of emotional intelligence and how emotional intelligence is measured.

What is emotional intelligence?

There are many definitions of emotional intelligence. In this chapter I briefly map two main strands and give an overview of the class of models one encounters. According to Joseph and Newman (2010), there are different types of models which describe the concept of emotional intelligence.

EI as an ability model

One well-researched model is based on a person's ability or intelligence. This model, originally proposed by Mayer et al. (2000), argues that EI is one of many types of intelligence and hence should be related to cognitive ability. A definition given by Salovey and Mayer (1990: 189) is that emotional intelligence is 'the ability to monitor one's own and others' feelings and emotions, to discriminate among them and to use this information to guide one's thinking and actions.' Mayer et al. (2008: 511) describe emotional intelligence as 'the ability to carry out accurate reasoning about emotions and the ability to use emotions and emotional knowledge to enhance thought'. As apparent in the definitions given, this model entails that emotional intelligence can be trained. Based on this idea, there are over 90 organizations (e.g. Joseph and Newman 2010) which are designed to assess and train people in emotional intelligence. Ability models conceptualize emotional intelligence as mental skills related to the accurate processing of emotion related information.

According to the ability model (Mayer and Salovey 1997), four 'emotion abilities', 'dimensions' or 'branches' are implicated. The first one is the ability to identify emotions accurately, express them and appraise them in self and others. This includes skills such as identifying and differentiating emotions based on bodily expressions, as well as feelings and thoughts, by self and other. A second ability concerns the capacity to use or generate emotions in order to facilitate or enhance cognitive functions, such as prioritizing information. A third factor concerns a linguistic understanding of the meaning of emotion such as labelling emotions accurately. The fourth dimension concerns managing emotions in self and others, such as reducing, enhancing or modifying emotional responses. In sum, each branch of the ability model describes a set of skills that make up overall emotional intelligence. Each branch has its own developmental trajectory, proceeding from relatively easy skills to more sophisticated ones. 'Perceiving emotions' according to this model typically begins with the ability to recognize basic emotions in faces and the pitch of voice or intonation contour. This ability develops and matures to the accurate perception of emotional blends as well as an ability to detect micro-expressions of emotions in the face.

In sum, the ability model emphasizes cognitive abilities when measuring emotional intelligence (e.g. Brackett and Geher 2006). Two tests that are widely used to measure emotional intelligence are the Multifactor Emotional Intelligence Scale (MEIS: Mayer et al. 1999) and the Mayer-Salovey-Caruso Emotional Intelligence Test (MSCEIT: Mayer et al. 2002). The MSCEIT defines EI as the ability to perceive, understand, use and manage emotions to facilitate thinking (Mayer et al. 2002). These tests are administered and assessed like an IQ test, comparing scores against correct answers from expert and general population norms. Other researchers argue not only that EI is a cognitive ability but also that personality factors influence EI results. These theories argue that EI needs to be conceived of as a mixed model.

EI as a mixed model

Research supporting a so-called mixed model argues that although cognitive ability does play a role in EI, it is a combination of cognitive ability, personality and emotion regulation. These mixed models are very broadly defined and hence are very difficult to test. So much so that some authors claim that there is a lack of empirical evidence for the construct of emotional intelligence (e.g. Murphy 2006). Furthermore, there are those researchers who believe that emotional intelligence is not different from other emotional constructs (e.g. Ciarrochi et al. 2002). According to Ciarrochi et al. (2002: 197), there is little empirical support for claims that emotional intelligence could predict life success or be advantageous in personal or professional development. In this critical view emotional intelligence is synonymous with general intelligence and in that sense relates for example to size of vocabulary, specifically, emotion words (e.g. Ciarrochi et al. 2002). At the other end of the spectrum, there are researchers who believe that EI is a personality trait and is unrelated to a person's ability.

The trait EI model

Trait emotional intelligence is defined as a constellation of self-perception which some authors argue is based on personality (e.g. Matthews et al. 2002). However, Petrides and colleagues argue (e.g. Petrides and Furnham 2003; Mavroveli et al. 2008) that trait emotional intelligence measures self-evaluations of constructs such as adaptability, emotion regulation, self-esteem and self-motivation. Mavroveli et al. (2008) argue that because trait EI is a personality construct, it should not correlate with cognitive abilities. The authors tested this hypothesis with a study of 139 11–12-year-old children (Mavroveli et al. 2008). As expected they found that 'trait EI was generally unrelated to academic performance' (Mavroveli et al. 2008: 520). This result was expected because conceptualizing EI as a trait rather than an ability means that it emphasizes the subjective nature of emotional experience (Watson 2000), which is a construct unrelated to human cognitive ability (Carroll 1993). However, the 'subjective' nature of this theory makes it difficult to measure objectively. This leads to the idea of some researchers that there is no such thing as emotional intelligence.

There is no such thing as emotional intelligence

Some authors query the utility of a concept of emotional intelligence. According to Locke (2005: 426), for example, 'the concept of EI has . . . become so broad and the components so variegated that no one concept could possible encompass or integrate all of them, no matter what the concept was called'; it is no longer even an intelligible concept. Locke asks (2005: 426): 'What is the common or integrating element in a concept that includes: introspection about emotions, emotional expression, non-verbal communication with others, empathy, self-regulation, planning, creative thinking and the direction of attention?' Instead Locke argues that emotions are automated processes which cannot be subjected to reasoning. Locke (2005: 427) summarized his view: 'one cannot, therefore, "reason with emotion;" one can only reason about it'.

Another problem with the concept of emotional intelligence is that the various scales used to measure it do not correlate. This implies that different scales test various aspects of the concept of emotional intelligence. Researchers who have opted for the ability model, in which high EI is reflected by emotion processing skills (e.g. Mayer et al. 1999, 2000), provide measuring scales which are based on objective tests measuring performance, whereas researchers subscribing to mixed models argue that EI comprises both abilities as well as a number of aspects of personal functioning. The Bar-On Emotional Quotient Inventory (EQ-I: Bar-On 2004) is a self-report measure, which assesses emotional and socially competent behaviour and purports to provide an estimate of a person's emotional and social intelligence. According to Bar-On (2004), the EQ-I is not designed to measure either personality traits or cognitive ability; rather it is designed to measure ability in terms of being able to successfully manage environmental demands and pressures. Hence the aim of these tests is to measure EI through self-report protocols and they are designed to assess beliefs and perceptions about an individual's competencies in specific domains (Salovey et al. 2001). The trait of EI is measured by tests which are seen by some to be similar to established personality tests, such as tests of the 'Big Five' personality traits (e.g. Eysenck 1967).

In spite of arguments against emotional intelligence, work published increases rather than decreases the areas to which EI measurements are applied. Originally the concept was used in business but now one finds widespread uses such as in education and health. Most research has focused on the positive or enhancing aspects of EI. However, high EI could also have negative or harmful effects.

Emotional intelligence is 'maladaptive'

There are some researchers who go so far as to write that emotional intelligence is maladaptive. In particular, Petrides and Sevdalis (2010: 527) argued that the conclusion that "'EQ is good for you'" . . . is almost certainly unwarranted', since it has been repeatedly demonstrated that there are circumstances and contexts where high EI scores are associated with maladaptive outcomes. For example, high EI individuals experience stronger negative emotions than their low EI peers when faced with a negative event (Sevdalis et al. 2007). High EI individuals are able to better manage stress or emotional expressions of others, which has been found in high EI people feeling happier and having better psychological health. There is indeed substantial evidence for the positive, life-enhancing aspects of EI (Furnham and Petrides 2003; Austin et al. 2005; Day et al. 2005). There is, however, also evidence for negative associations of EI with stress, proneness to depression and loneliness (Slaski and Cartwright 2002; Saklofske et al. 2003). Additionally there is the potentially negative aspect of high EI in a person who uses high EI abilities to manipulate others' emotions for their own rather than the other person's benefit (e.g. de Raad 2005).

In sum, trait EI theory, according to Petrides et al. (2007), explicitly rejects models that view EI as a cognitive ability and instead it is seen as a constellation of emotion-related self-perceptions. Being subjective, this perception of emotions can only have value for each person's specific circumstance and context (Petrides et al. 2007). This subjective aspect of EI implies that not only is it difficult to measure EI objectively, but also a person with high trait EI might have not only heightened positive but also heightened negative experiences (Austin et al. 2007).

How is emotional intelligence measured?

A number of tests have been developed for both the ability type of emotional intelligence and the trait type of emotional intelligence. Ability emotional intelligence is measured by an ability scale such as the Mayer-Salovey-Caruso Emotional Intelligence Test. The MSCEIT can evaluate individual differences in the four processes stipulated in the Mayer-Salovey-Caruso ability model of EI. Differences that exist between those people who are more or less able to accurately perceive how a story protagonist might feel, by identifying feelings expressed in the face and body postures are measured with the MSCEIT. This test is operationalized formally as a set of problems for each of the four branches. The responses which are given by a person taking the test are compared with a criterion of 'correct' or 'false' response. The MSCEIT consists of eight tasks, two for each of the four branches of the EI model (Mayer et al. 1999, 2002, 2003).

Additionally, there are a number of ability-based scales of emotional 'perception', which is just one branch of the four branch model. For example, Matsumoto and Ekman's Japanese and Caucasian Brief Affect Recognition Test (JACBART) measures individual differences in recognizing emotions in Japanese and Caucasian faces (Matsumoto et al. 2000).

Other researchers compared measures of ability EI with measures of trait EI. For example Brannick et al. (2009) compared the results of two different EI measures, administered to medical students, namely an ability measure, the MSCEIT, and a trait measure, using the self-report format of the Wong and Law Emotional Intelligence Scale (WLEIS). The aim of this study was to compare the two scales with measures of the Big Five personality traits in order to ascertain whether the two measures would yield similar or different results. It was argued that if the two scales yielded different results, this would provide evidence that EI measures different aspects of personality than are assessed with routine personality tests. The Big Five personality traits were measured by the Neuroticism-Extroversion-Openness (NEO) test. Brannick et al. (2009) found that the ability measure (MSCEIT) yielded unreliable results. More interestingly, the MSCEIT had a very low correlation of 0.18 with the WLEIS. Furthermore the WLEIS was more highly correlated with personality scales than the MSCEIT. Hence, this demonstrates that there are two different types of EI, namely an aspect of emotional intelligence which relates to ability and one which relates to personality.

The following chapters discuss emotional intelligence in relation to a number of areas in which they have been studied. Chapter 3 reviews studies on the language of emotional intelligence, including para-linguistic aspects such as pitch voice, demonstrating that emotional intelligence is fostered from the first days of an infant's life. Chapter 4 discusses issues of the regulation of emotional intelligence in a social context, including the effects of maternal mental health on infant emotional development. Chapter 5 concerns the role of empathy in the development of emotional intelligence. Finally Chapter 6 discusses the effects of negative emotions of self and other in relation to emotionally intelligent functioning. For example, how can psychiatric nurses who have to work with violent patients cope with the negative emotions generated in their workplace?

3   The language of emotional intelligence

People report their emotions by using words. In polite society a person asks: 'How are you?' Or 'How are you feeling today?' The response is emotionally charged, such as the person is 'feeling' well or sometimes not so well. However, verbal reports might not accurately represent what the person is feeling. I review the literature selectively concentrating wherever possible on studies involving infants rather than adults.

People vary in how accurately they distinguish between emotions, as a study showed in which individuals had to rate their current emotional state (Feldman-Barrett et al. 2001). In this study participants had to report how closely the emotion terms of, for example, happy, elated, anxious or annoyed described how they currently felt. Some participants had strong correlations between feeling states of the same valence. These people seemed to distinguish between positive or negative emotions but they did not differentiate between various positive (e.g. happy, elated) or negative (anxious, annoyed) emotions. Feldman-Barrett (2004) developed a method to assess how well people can describe their emotions. Some people are said to have only a vague idea of their emotional state, using either positive or negative global terms to describe how they feel, such as feeling good or bad. However, other people are able to define how they feel in much more specific ways, such as feeling elated or despondent. These people who use specific terms that are able to convey fine differences between emotional states are said to be high in emotional granularity. In contrast people who can give only vague descriptions of their current state are said to be low in emotional granularity. Feldman-Barrett (2004) argued that people low in granularity, in comparison with people high in granularity, might either differentiate fewer emotional experiences or they might have a poorer semantic understanding of emotion words. Their results indicated that self-reported ratings of emotions are more than a semantic under-standing of the vocabulary. They also reported that those people who focused more on the valence of the emotion, positive or negative, rather than the strength of arousal elicited by the emotion, were able to process facial expressions more sensitively. The researchers con-cluded that 'although self report ratings might be influenced by individual differences in emotion vocabulary, they are not solely determined by them' (Feldman-Barrett 2004: 279). Indeed, in one study (Durbin 2010) children between 3 and 6 years of age were tested on their vocabulary and their ability to identify fear, sadness, anger, happiness, surprise and neutral emotions. There was only a weak effect of emotion word knowledge and identifying children's own emotions in structured laboratory tasks. In this study, in order to elicit happiness, children were told that they could decorate a T-shirt with paints and take it home and then were asked how they felt. In order to elicit fear, a stranger approached the children speaking to them in a neutral tone of voice. Contrary to expectations there were no significant age differences in reporting emotions; nor was there a significant difference between children with emotion word knowledge and children who knew fewer emotion words. Specifically, children's self-reports of positive or negative emotions felt in the laboratory tasks were unrelated to their vocabulary scores achieved on the Peabody Picture Vocabulary Test (Dunn and Dunn 1997). Hence, children's verbal intelligence was unrelated to their self-reported emotional state knowledge. If children do not rely on verbal knowl-edge, they might just rely on facial expressions to identify different emotions.

Recognizing emotions in facial expressions: is there a developmental progression?

Some work suggests that children rely on facial expression to identify emotions. This is the conclusion of studies examining babies at the preverbal stage in terms of their ability to identify degrees of one emotion, namely happiness (e.g. Bornstein and Arterberry 2003). Bornstein and Arterberry (2003) argued that recognizing emotions correctly is fundamental for the development of interpersonal skills. Development of this ability is vital for emotional signal exchange when verbal communication is very limited (e.g. Papoušek and Papoušek 2002). It is in fact the basis for emotionally intelligent functioning and is tested as part of emotional intelligence tests. Bornstein and Arterberry (2003), testing 5-month-old infants, found that they were able to discriminate not only between smiles and fearful expressions, but also between smile intensity. Four degrees of smiling were modelled by either the same or a different person. Results showed that the 5 month olds were able to recognize whether the emotions were modelled by the same or a different person and they were able to discriminate between emotion intensity. However, more recent work indicates that happiness seems to be a special emotion. Gao and Maurer (2010) tested happiness, fear, surprise, neutral, sadness, disgust, and anger in children at 5, 7 and 10 years of age and a comparison group of adults. In contrast to previous studies using photographic displays of emotions, usually posed by trained actors who are instructed to use prescribed muscle movements (e.g., Pictures of Facial Affect: Ekman and Friesen 1976), this study tested the intensity of emotional displays. Specifically, this study tested not only whether participants could distinguish between various emotions but also at what point they could say that an emotion displayed was different from neutral. They were asked to categorize for example a smile with intensities varying from 0 per cent, namely a neutral expression, to 100 per cent (peak) a big grin. Previous studies asked children to label prototypical emotion expressions of high intensity. Results indicated that children show a large improvement in accuracy in tasks requiring matching or labelling between 3 and 7 years of age (e.g. Camras and Allison 1985; Vicari et al. 2000; Durand et al. 2007). There are also different developmental trajectories for different expression categories, with positive expressions being recognized earlier and more accurately than negative expressions (e.g. Camras and Allison 1985; Vicari et al. 2000; Widen and Russell 2003; Durand et al. 2007).

In sum, the developmental course using photographs of prototypical expressions of peak intensity from different emotion categories resulted in the findings that children aged 3 years show a large improvement in accuracy in tasks requiring matching or labelling (Camras and Allison 1985; Durand et al. 2007). Furthermore, positive expressions are recognized earlier and more accurately than negative expressions (e.g. Vicari et al. 2000; Widen and Russell 2003). Gao and Maurer (2010) argued that although photographs of intense expressions are a useful tool to study the development of the recognition of facial expressions, these intense expressions are not usually encountered in everyday life. Hence, they tested children 5, 7 and 10 years of age and a comparison group of adults on their recognition of emotions varying in intensity. Their results, in accordance with other research, indicated that for happiness, even 5 year olds were able to identify happiness from a very low level of intensity. Hence, even the slightest indication of a smile was recognized by these young children. Anger closely followed happiness in terms of ease of identification. All age groups had perfect accuracy at peak intensity of the expression of anger. For sad expressions the picture was less clear. Although with intensity of sad expression, accuracy increased with age, 7 year olds were less accurate in comparison with 5 and 10 year olds. It was unclear why 7 year olds showed this lack in differentiating the sad emotion. Regarding fear, 7 and 10 year olds performed similarly to adults. However, 5-year-old children had more difficulties in identifying fearful faces than the adults. The other emotion not well identified was disgust, in that 5–7 year olds misidentified disgusted faces as sad (5 year olds) or neutral (7 year olds). Surprise was least well identified. Even adults made mistakes. At peak intensity of surprise only 54 per cent of the 5 year olds and 77 per cent of adults identified the emotion correctly.

One reason for these results could be that it is not the intensity of the facial expression but the vocal expression accompanying the emotion which helps to differentiate for example surprise from happiness. Additionally, sensitivity to emotional prosody or intonation contour might distinguish between those people scoring high or low in emotional intelligence. The idea that music and the syntax of language have a common basis has been suggested by Patel (2003). Even more closely related to music is the pitch or melody of voice when speaking. So much so that preverbal infants listen to the pitch of voice and react to that before they understand the semantic content of words used. In one study (Reissland and Shepherd 2002) infants aged 3, 5 and 9 months were video- and audiotaped during surprise-eliciting play with a Jack-in-the-box and play with a soft toy. Maternal and infant gaze direction as well as their facial expressions of surprise, fear, pleasure and neutral were coded. Additionally, maternal exclamations of surprise were compared with similar vocalizations during a non-surprising play situation. This study found that mothers adjusted their pitch of voice depending on whether or not their infants looked at their face. Mothers whose baby looked at her while the Jack-in-the-box opened exclaimed surprise with a higher pitch (mean pitch: 411 Hz) in comparison with mothers whose child looked at the Jack-in-the-box (mean pitch: 358 Hz). Additionally, infants reacted to maternal pitch of voice before they reacted to their mothers' facial surprise expression.

Hence when trying to understand the language of emotional intelligence in a developmental framework, we might need to look first at the melody of language which expresses emotions. Do you need to be musical in order to show high emotional intelligence?

Pitch of voice and emotional intelligence

Although popular programmes teach emotional intelligence, there is very little academic research on the relation between the pitch of voice and emotional intelligence. One programme talks about how 'The sound of your voice conveys your moment-to-moment emotional experience' and how this can be trained as part of the training in emotional intelligence. It is generally accepted that human speech provides information about the emotional states of a person through the acoustic properties of speech (e.g., Bachorowski 1999). These are measured by the fundamental frequency of speech (F0). The F0 corresponds to the rate of vocal-fold vibration and is perceived as vocal pitch. Most research has been focused on the hypothesis that distinct acoustic patterns are associated with various emotions. Experimental investigations concerned mostly neutral sentences spoken with various emotional expressions. The results of these studies (e.g. Scherer et al. 1991; Banse and Scherer 1996; Leinonen et al. 1997) showed that when analysing mean pitch of voice (F0) and amplitude measured in decibels, fear, joy and anger were defined by higher mean pitch than emotionally neutral vocalizations whereas sadness was associated with a comparatively lower mean pitch. In order to distinguish between high energy emotions (e.g. joy or anger) the researchers discovered that one needed to analyse the contours of F0 changes. For example F0 increases over time when joy is expressed but the pitch contour of anger decreases over time. The findings of previous studies have mostly related to active or passive emotions or positive and negative affective states.

There are a number of studies which have found that newborn babies hearing cries of other newborns will start to cry, which has been interpreted as showing this might be the very earliest stages of a development of empathy. Geangu et al. (2010) examined the reactions of 1, 3, 6 and 9 month olds to recordings of infant cries. Their results indicated that during the presentation of a pain cry sound, 1, 3, 6 and 9 month olds manifested increased vocal and facial expressions of distress. Furthermore, negative reactions did not decrease with age. Additionally, boys and girls manifested similar levels of anger when hearing a pain cry of another infant. According to Geangu et al. (2010), these results suggest that the emotional reactions to the perception of another infant cry is the result of emotional contagion, rather than reactions to aversive sounds.

Szameitat et al. (2009) investigated one specific emotional expression, namely laughter, but distinguished between different types of laughter. They argued that although listeners are able to decode the underlying emotions embedded in acoustical laughter sounds of joy, tickling, taunting and *schadenfreude*, little is known about the acoustical cues that differentiate between these emotions. Their study was designed to investigate the acoustic correlates of these different types of laughter by analysing forty-three acoustic parameters. They were able to show that prosodic parameters were most effective in differentiating between the four types of laughter. Verbally expressed emotions, according to the author, are expressed by similar prosodic parameters.

Pell (2001) examined the specifics of prosodic parameters. The study was designed to identify in sentences of varying length, either six syllables or ten syllables long, in terms of sad, happy or angry emotions expressed. Pell (2001) found that the emotion's intonation was pronounced for specific content words and that these key words marked the sentence in terms of the emotion expressed.

The ability to recognize and decode emotions increases with normal development. There is some research indicating that older adults are less able to recognize negative emotions; specifically anger and sadness were less well recognized by this group. In contrast, the positive emotions of happiness and surprise were well recognized by all age groups (e.g. Isaacowitz et al. 2007). This is in contrast to Gao and Maurer (2010), who found that although adults were better at recognizing all emotions, in general negative emotions are less well decoded by the young and adults.

Another study compared nonverbal, verbal and facial stimuli in order to identify whether participants were able to identify emotional content better from nonverbal vocal stimuli or from facial expressions (Hawk et al. 2009). Participants were asked to identify ten emotional expressions, including anger, contempt, disgust, fear, sadness, embarrassment, surprise, joy, pride and 'neutral'. The results showed that participants in this study identified the nonsense sounds of anger, contempt, disgust, fear, sadness and surprise, better than facial expressions of these emotions. In contrast, the facial expressions displaying 'neutral' or no emotions as well as embarrassment, joy and pride were better recognized from emotional displays rather than sounds. The identification of emotions based on intonation of spoken sentences seemed much more difficult and the conclusion was that speakers convey emotional messages through other channels (Hawk et al. 2009).

In sum, it seems that emotions are recognized in a number of different ways, namely through the melody of vocalization, facial expression and to a lesser extent the ability to label emotions.

However, these studies have not examined how children develop in a social context in which they learn about other people's emotions as well as their own. The next chapter will examine the differentiation between self and other and how this might affect the child's under-standing of emotions and the development of emotionally intelligent functioning.

4 Regulation of emotional expression

An integral part of emotional intelligence concerns the ability to regulate one's emotions. This chapter examines the development of a concept of self and the impact on self and self-regulation as well as awareness and management of others' emotions.

Among the many models of emotional functioning is the component process model of emotions developed by Scherer (2009), which includes the self-concept as one factor. Scherer and Ellgring (2007) propose that the component process model of emotional intelligence captures the complexity of emotion including cognition, motivation, physiological reaction and motor expression. The central mechanism for emotion generation is the appraisal of events. Appraisal drives the type of emotional reactions produced by an event in terms of factors such as novelty, pleasantness, goal conduciveness, significance of the event and the coping potential of a person. The authors give as an example anger, which

> is expected to be the result of an event being appraised as an obstruction to reaching a goal or satisfying a need, produced by an unfair intentional act of another person, that could be removed by powerful action, with a correspondent response patterning consisting of aggressive action tendencies, involving sympathetic arousal, knitted brows, square mouth with teeth clenched, and loud, strident vocal utterances.
>
> (Scherer and Ellgring 2007: 159)

The model of emotional intelligence proposed by Scherer (2009) includes the ability to monitor and regulate feelings. The development of this ability has been investigated by a number of researchers under the heading of emotional competence. Emotional competence entails not only knowledge of emotions, including labelling emotions and situations which elicit certain emotions, but also the ability to regulate emotions (e.g. Eisenberg et al. 1998). Emotional competence has been defined as

> an understanding of one's own and others' emotions, the tendency to display emotion in a situationally and culturally appropriate manner, and the ability to inhibit or modulate experienced and expressed emotion and emotionally derived behaviour as needed to achieve goals in a socially acceptable manner.
>
> (Eisenberg et al. 1998: 242)

Sensitivity to the emotions of others is essential for normal development. According to Trevarthen (2001), it is from the first days and weeks of life that infants respond sympathetically to emotions by engaging in face-to-face intersubjective communication, which enables them to express their own intentions and emotional states to others as well as respond to the emotions and intentions expressed by others.

The development of infant emotional sensitivity has been investigated in different areas, including the effects of maternal depressed mood in the postnatal period. Depressed mothers often show difficulties in engaging their infants. This is due to the fact that depressed mothers are less sensitive and responsive (e.g. Field et al. 1990; Murray 1992; Dumas et al. 2001). Even though depressed mothers might not show their depression overtly (Frankel and Harmon 1996), infants are sensitive to their depressed mother's behaviours and react by disengaging from the mother. In one study infants of depressed and non-depressed mothers were observed while reading a picture book (Reissland and Burt 2010). In this study, the babies of depressed mothers were reluctant to engage with their mothers in this task; they pushed the book away or even tried to close it, preventing their mothers from reading the book. In contrast, babies of non-depressed mothers enjoyed looking at the picture book. These types of problematic interactions between depressed mothers and their infants lead to more negative emotional expressions, disturbances in attention, and less efficient processing of contingent relationships (Beebe et al. 2008).

Regulation of emotions is a learned process which occurs in the context of socializing children into their cultural environment (e.g. Saarni 2001). Parents play a major role in this socialization process, especially at a young age. Eisenberg et al. (1998) reviewed parental socialization of emotion and argued that one way in which one can observe and evaluate parental socialization techniques is to focus research on parental reactions to children's experience and expression of emotions. They argue that parental reactions to children's emotions play a major role in the child's socialization into expressing and managing their own emotions.

Self-regulation of emotions in infancy

Not all infants are the same. The difference between infants has been conceptualized in terms of infant temperament. Infant irritability and ability to be soothed, for example, depends on not only the mother's but also her infant's disposition. Research on crying emphasizes these differences. For example, research examined individual differences of mothers and their infants, aged 2 and 6 months, in a longitudinal study (Jahromi and Stifter 2007). Although the intensity of crying in response to inoculation varied over time, the durations of the cry response by each of the infants was relatively stable. The authors suggest that this might be due to maternal soothing techniques, employing emotion, touching and vocalizing, which showed the strongest stability across infant age. The results of this study indicate that infants at an early age are socialized into how to express and manage their emotions. This is reflected in the finding of the study that infants whose mothers were able to reduce their infants' pain expressions to a greater extent at 2 months cried for a shorter duration at 6 months compared with infants of mothers who were less able to reduce their infants' pain expression at 2 months of age. Mothers will usually adapt their emotional reactions to their infants' developmental maturity. With 2-month-old infants, mothers use more affection and touching, whereas 6-month-old infants are soothed through maternal vocalizations and distraction (e.g. Jahromi et al. 2004).

Research on the development of attachment indicates that maternal methods of soothing their distressed infants are not only important in terms of regulation of current infant emotions but also vital for the later development of children's ability to regulate their own emotions. Part of the emotion regulation mechanism early in life depends on maternal modelling of emotional expressions (e.g. Malatesta and Haviland 1982; Reissland 1990, 1994). The other part comes from the child. Specifically, infants' ability to control attention, soothe themselves and to withdraw are behaviours which can be observed before infants have reached 6 months of age (e.g. Crockenberg and Leerkes 2004).

Mothers are able to reduce their infants' negative experiences by behaviours such as touch, distraction and positive emotions and by swaddling, which reduce infant pain expressions (e.g., Grolnick et al. 1998). However, mothers who show negative emotional expressions themselves have children who show more distress (e.g. Hornik et al. 1987). The fact that maternal behaviour influences her infant's expression of distress has been shown experimentally. In one study (Crockenberg and Leerkes 2004) 6-month-old infants were observed with their mothers while watching two novel toys. In one condition mothers were asked not to engage with the child and in the second condition they were asked to engage with their baby as they liked. The researchers measured infant emotional displays as well as regulatory behaviours. Results showed that 6-month-old babies are capable of reducing their own distress by soothing themselves as well as looking away from the novel toy. Furthermore, mothers supported their infants' regulatory behaviours by responding to their babies' attention cues; when the baby looked away then the mother looked away. Hence, mothers foster infants' ability to regulate their distress.

However, what happens if mothers have problems regulating their own emotions, such as the case when mothers have mental health problems?

The effects of maternal mental health as the basis for emotional intelligence

There is some consensus that maternal mental health has an effect on children's emotional development (e.g. Murray et al. 1993; Reissland and Shepherd 2006). Specifically, in young children who do not yet have the ability to differentiate the self from the other, the influences of the caregiver are pronounced. Furthermore, maternal mental health problems are related to children's attachment status. Specifically, insecurely attached children are known to be at greater risk of emotional problems, such as deficits in emotional understanding, later on (Green and Goldwyn 2002). Most research has concentrated on depression. This research has established (e.g. Cicchetti et al. 1998) that depressed mothers compared with non-depressed mothers have toddlers who are more insecurely attached. Additionally, there is some work (e.g. Manassis et al. 1994) which suggests that maternal anxiety disorders affect children, who show insecure attachments to these mothers. Early attachment, in terms of infants developing emotional competence, relates to dyadic affect regulation (e.g. Sroufe 1997). This regulation between mother and infant allows infants to manage emotions with the help of their mothers. Especially, responsive and sensitive mothers who provide well-coordinated structures when interacting with their babies, compared with unresponsive mothers, have infants who show improved emotion regulation. Belsky et al. (1991) were able to show that if 3-month-old infants interacted with sensitive mothers, they expressed fewer negative and more positive emotions at 9 months of age. Additionally they found that infants expressing more positive compared with infants expressing more negative emotions during play were more likely to be rated securely attached at 12 months. Various studies have suggested that early attachment styles can predict children's emotionality. One author (Kochanska 2001) argued that, based on present research, one can make a number of predictions of different patterns of emotional development depending on the early attachment histories of children. According to Kochanska (2001), avoidant attachment might lead to reduced expressions of sadness, fear or anger and possibly increased positive affect. In contrast, resistant attachment might be character-ized by increased expressions of negative emotions. The emotion regulation of insecure children was hypothesized to be more complex. Avoidant children are expected to be more variable in their expres-sions of emotions depending on the person they interact with. The engagement of unresponsive caregivers with a baby who is dependent on the carer for their emotional response leads to the development of anxiety in young children (e.g. Chorpita and Barlow 1998) and is long lasting. Anxiety disorders in adults are related to their early experi-ences with a carer who, because for example of having experienced a traumatic event such as divorce, conflict or death, is incapable of providing a secure base (e.g. Kendler et al. 1992). An adult who is still suffering depression because of a divorce or because of conflict in the family might not have the ability to attend to the child adequately. This insensitive behaviour might result in the child feeling insecure and hence not becoming securely attached to the adult. Lewis and Feiring (1991) found that children growing up in families where they experienced conflict showed more signs of psychopathology compared with children raised in happy families.

In sum, securely attached children of healthy mothers are able to develop emotionally such that they can show emotional intelligence in their interactions later on. The question is: how do parents socialize positive emotions and self-awareness in their children?

Socialization of positive emotions

Most infants will be happy when they are close to their carer, who will hold them when the child feels the need to be held (Bell and

Ainsworth 1972). However, it is not always possible for a parent to assent to the child's requests. In that case parents have to regulate infant behaviour and children have to learn to comply with requests. Parents who use positive controlling strategies guide their children in finding ways to cope with difficult situations themselves. They reward successful self-regulation and this supports the development of self-regulation in these children (Putnam et al. 2002). Negative controlling strategies, on the other hand, might result in inadequate self-regulation. However, it is not only parental control but also the way children themselves behave. Children who are able to show some ability in self-regulation not only elicit more parental guidance but also benefit from parental guidance. Children, who lack the skills of self-regulation skills, oblige their parents to enhance their power by controlling infant behaviour (Kochanska and Aksan 1995).

According to Putnam et al. (2002), the development of children's ability to control their own behaviour is dependent on how well they can cope with the competing demands of internal desires and external constraints. The main aim of socializing children into their cultural milieu is to support children to delay immediate gratification so that they can gain social approval, which also forms an important part in the development of the fostering emotional intelligence. This can be seen by the fact that the inability to delay gratification is correlated with low peer ratings, tendencies to respond to social problem situations with aggression, and insufficient use of social and emotional cues (Mischel et al. 1988). Hence, a lack of self-control early in childhood predicts behaviour disorders later on.

Mischel et al. (1988) found that if children were unable to delay their gratification when they were pre-schoolers, they showed poor academic, social and coping skills as adolescents. According to Putnam et al. (2002), the increasing ability to delay gratification is due to children's developing strategies. Such strategies include attending to items which are not prohibited rather than focusing on the prohibited item. Few 4-year-old children will acknowledge that distraction helps whereas nearly all 8 year olds recognize the value of focusing on other stimuli as a strategy to facilitate waiting; nevertheless, even toddlers seem to have a rudimentary understanding that distraction might help them to cope with waiting (Cournoyer and Trudel 1991). According to Fredrickson (1998), three types of parenting behaviours contribute to children's emotional competence: first, the ability of parents to regulate and express their own emotions appropriately; second, the way parents react to their children's emotional expressions; third, the coaching of emotional expressions with younger children and discussions about their emotions with older children. Parental expressions of positive emotions as well as their ability to support children's appropriate expressions of negative emotions are vital for children's healthy emotional development. Specifically talking about emotions, in terms of labelling emotions and explaining causes and consequences of emotions leads to enhanced socio-emotional competence in children. This competence can be couched in terms of enhanced emotional intelligence in that it leads to the better understanding of emotions, awareness of one's own and others' emotions and the ability to regulate emotion. In contrast, according to Fredrickson (1998), parents' negative, unsupportive practices (e.g. punitive or minimizing) in response to children's expression of negative emotions can have a negative effect on children's socio-emotional functioning and are linked to lower levels of emotional knowledge, and lower emotion regulation ability.

In sum, the ability to regulate emotions is a fundamental aspect of healthy emotional functioning and plays an important role in the development of emotional intelligence from infancy onward. The way in which one can conceptualize this development is further discussed in the case study in the second part of this book, where I show how the emotions in the context of dressing the baby change over time.

5 Emotional intelligence
The ability to interact emotionally through empathy

Part of emotional intelligence is the ability to recognize emotions in others, that is to be empathetic to others. One definition of empathy is 'the knowledge and sharing of others' feelings', which is essential for the development of prosocial behaviour (Knafo et al. 2009: 103).

The development of empathy

Empathy helps one person to relate to the emotional state of another quickly and automatically, initially without reliance on cognitive processes (Hoffman 1981). This ability to access others' emotions quickly is fundamental in terms of the management of social interactions, coordinated activity, and cooperation to achieve shared goals. The lowest common denominator of all empathic processes, according to de Waal (2008), is that one person is affected by another's emotional or arousal state, namely emotional contagion.

Emotional bonds between mother and child start early, often before birth. This has led to research on maternal fetal attachment defined as 'the extent to which women engage in behaviours that represent an affiliation and interaction with their unborn child' (Cranley 1981: 282). This prenatal attachment, formed by the mother initially, is reciprocated early after birth (e.g. Zahn-Waxler and Radke-Yarrow 1990). At this first stage of emotional bonding or attachment between mother and child, one can speak of 'emotional contagion' (de Waal 2008). One can find emotional contagion, not only in the attachment between mother and child but also for example in the cry of the newborn baby, who cries when he or she hears another baby cry in the nursery.

Theories propose that emotional contagion occurs quickly, within 500ms, in response to seeing emotional facial expressions. For a negative facial expression the corrugator supercilii is activated to produce a frown and for a positive facial expression the zygomaticus major is activated producing a smile (e.g. Dimberg and Thunberg 1998). Not only does seeing a facial expression of emotion lead to emotional contagion, but also hearing sounds relates to how newborn babies behave. Specifically, research with babies listening to either their own cry sound or the crying of another baby, established that even 1-day-old babies are able to discriminate between their own and other infants' cries. Furthermore, this research showed that the cry of a newborn baby is highly effective in inducing distress responses in another newborn infant (e.g. Dondi et al. 1999).

The second stage of emotional bonding is called 'sympathetic concern', in which appraisal of the other's situation and attempts to understand the cause of the other's emotions is added to emotional contagion. Sympathy, defined as an affective response which concerns feelings of sadness, consists of feelings of apprehension for a distressed other rather than sharing the emotion of the other. Sympathy is believed to involve an 'other-oriented, altruistic motivation' (Eisenberg 2000: 677). De Waal (1996) calls this stage also 'cognitive empathy' because the empathic reaction includes an additional factor, namely the appraisal of the context. Concern for others necessitates the ability to differentiate between internally and externally generated emotions. This separation can already be observed in very young children. One study (Zahn-Waxler et al. 1984), of 1-year-old babies' responses to family members, who were instructed to pretend to be sad by crying, found that the babies tried to comfort the distressed person, by, for example, putting their head in the lap of that person.

The third stage is 'empathic perspective taking'. Perspective taking itself is a cognitive ability, in the sense of being able to understand another's point of view. This is also called 'theory of mind'. Theory of mind can be tested with the so-called false belief tasks. In such a task two children, Sally and Ann, observe one object being hidden in Box A. Ann leaves the room and the object is moved from Box A to Box B. Sally is asked where will Ann look for the object when she returns. Younger children say that it will be Box B, even though Ann could not have observed the changing location of the object from Box A to Box B. Older children do not make such mistakes. In one study, Astington and Jenkins (1999) found that language abilities earlier in childhood predict later false belief performance in theory of mind tasks. However, false belief competence earlier in childhood does not predict later language abilities, supporting the conclusion that language is a necessary precursor to social cognitive development as measured by theory of mind tasks. Bloom and German (2000) argued that even though 3 year olds do not seem able to pass the false belief tasks, which usually test theory of mind capability, there are other tests which have demonstrated that even children younger than 3 years of age can reason about other people's state of mind. In one study 2-year-old children were tested with parents either present or absent. These 2 year olds observed an experimenter place an attractive toy on a high shelf which they could not reach without help. When the parents returned to the room, children whose parents did not witness the toy being placed on the high shelf gestured more and named the toy more often compared with the children whose parents had witnessed the experimenter place the toy on the shelf. The different behaviours observed suggest to Bloom and German (2000) that even 2 year olds modify their behaviour according to the states of knowledge they perceive other people to have, namely that the parent either knew or did not know that the toy was placed on the shelf. Furthermore, Bloom and German (2000) argued that this demonstrated that 2 year olds have a tacit appreciation of the circumstances under which beliefs are formed. This appreciation is cognitive. However, empathetic perspective taking involves emotional engagement and not only purely cognitive abilities. This is a more difficult task in that children need to understand that the emotions induced in them are in fact due to how the other person feels. In order to be able to perform such a task children need, according to Lewis (2002), a representation of the self as part of the representation 'we'; otherwise young children do not show empathy which is supported by cognition, specifically cognition about self, which is a meta-representational ability. According to Lewis (2002: 42), 'this developmental sequence, going from social reflexes, such as contagion, to cognitions, such as self-representation, constitutes an important shift in the human child's development'.

In sum, research points to the fact that in order to show emotional intelligence one needs both intellectual and perspective taking abilities which develop over time, as the neonate moves to the infant and toddler stages of development. However, there is one group of children who present with problems here, namely children on the autistic spectrum.

Trait and ability EI and empathy

A primary characteristic of people with Asperger syndrome is that although they develop typically in terms of their cognitive and language skills, they lack age-appropriate social abilities (e.g. Gutstein and Whitney 2002). Asperger syndrome is a complex condition, which has attracted a lot of research. Part of the complexity of this syndrome relates to the definition of what it is. According to Khouzam et al. (2004), Asperger syndrome is on the autistic spectrum and includes social behaviours, restricted interests and repetitive behaviours which in contrast to autism are usually diagnosed after 3 years of age. Children diagnosed with Asperger syndrome show normal intellectual function and language development but apparent motor clumsiness. These social and emotional problems can have a major impact on the social life of people with Asperger symdrome, who may have difficulties in understanding the implicit rules of socialization and lack empathy (Wing 1981). Furthermore, research has established that the social difficulties of people with Asperger syndrome relate to their inability to evaluate social cues appropriately, which is necessary for empathetic perspective taking, and to engage in correct behaviours, such as following the social conventions of the cultural context in which they find themselves. According to Montgomery et al. (2010), the construct of emotional intelligence as an ability and a trait could illuminate the problems which individuals with Asperger syndrome encounter.

Although there is some controversy surrounding both the ability and trait models of EI (as discussed in Chapter 2) at least some research has demonstrated the validity of each of the models in areas relating to social skills. The trait EI model predicts successful social interaction (e.g. Lopes et al. 2005) and the ability model of EI has been shown to positively correlate with self-reported empathy (e.g. Ciarrochi et al. 2000) and social competence (e.g. Brackett et al. 2006). Given that social interaction can be difficult for people with Asperger syndrome and that they may also have difficulty in showing empathy, Montgomery et al. (2010) examined EI, both trait and ability, in a group of 16–21 year olds diagnosed with Asperger syndrome.

The participants were given a valid and reliable self-report measure, testing their trait EI, namely the Bar-On Emotional Quotient Inventory – Computer Administered Version, short form (Bar-On EQ-IS: Bar-On 2002). The measure of 51 questions tests, for example, how a person perceives their stress management, how adaptable they are, and their mood. Additionally it tests whether participants see themselves as creating more positive impressions than is true in reality. Montgomery et al. (2010) found that the people with Asperger syndrome, compared with a group not having the syndrome, performed significantly worse. The Asperger syndrome group, compared with a normative sample, had significantly lower scores than the normative group on the Intrapersonal, Interpersonal, Stress Management and

General Mood scales of the Bar-On test. Particularly, Montgomery et al. (2010) pointed out that the Asperger syndrome group tended to report positively about their own EI, although their scores on the test were lower than the mean scores for the normative group. Given that it is a self-report test, this implies that the values provided may actually underestimate the extent of difficulties.

In order to test their ability EI, the group of Asperger syndrome participants were given the Mayer-Salovey-Caruso Emotional Intelligence Test (Mayer et al. 2002), which is derived from the four-branch model of EI proposed by Mayer et al. (2001). This test gives results for Emotional Experience and Emotional Reasoning, which reflect the performance in the four areas of the theoretical model, namely the ability to perceive emotions, use emotions in order to facilitate thought, understand emotions, and manage emotions in order to foster personal growth and healthy social relations. On this ability measure, the participants with Asperger syndrome performed to the same standard as the normative group, except in the Understanding Emotions branch of the MSCEIT. Here participants with Asperger syndrome performed significantly better than the normative group. According to Montgomery et al. (2010), this result is consistent with reports for this group on tasks from a similar construct, theory of mind. In studies examining the ability to reason about other people's thoughts, feelings and perceptions, different individuals with Asperger syndrome are able to complete laboratory tasks when they have enough time to think about the situation theoretically (Baron-Cohen et al. 1997). In contrast, when they have to act out in real-life scenarios, they perform poorly (Dissanayake and Macintosh 2003). This has been found by a number of researchers, who argue that participants with Asperger syndrome use their verbal skills to reason through the cognitive aspects of a scenario or problem involving emotional perspective taking. However, these same people do much worse when having to perform in a naturalistic situation (Dissanayake and Macintosh 2003). Hence the results of Montgomery et al. (2010) suggest that individuals with Asperger syndrome have good knowledge about how to reason through emotionally based scenarios, tested with the ability EI, especially when they have enough time to process information and evaluate various options.

EI and understanding jokes

Understanding humour has been linked to social competence, popularity and adaptability, which are all measured by emotional intelligence. Hence, one can expect a relation between EI ability and appreciation of jokes. Parents engage in humorous interactions with their children from infancy, as can be seen in the case study in the second part of this book. Humorous situations, according to Kappas (1967), include elements of incongruity. By associating incompatible features, situations are perceived as humorous. Incongruity, to various degrees, is the basis of all forms of humour. According to Zigler et al. (1966), understanding any particular joke may require a variety of cognitive processes, including the ability to comprehend unusual verbal representations. The pleasure is derived from the cognitive work which needs to be done in order to understand the joke. Pinderhughes and Zigler (1985) analysed the development of children's understanding of humour, comparing children aged between 5 and 10 years, rated on their intelligence, with their comprehension of jokes and ratings of degrees of funniness of the jokes. As expected, the more difficult jokes were perceived to be funnier by the older children. Additionally, IQ was significantly correlated with understanding of the jokes.

If humour is based on the genetic make-up (e.g. Darwin 1872), one would expect people with Asperger syndrome compared to the general population to perform worse in understanding humour. Furthermore, given that people with Asperger syndrome intellectualize the world, they might appreciate one type of humour based on logic, patterns or rules, such as humour in mathematics (e.g. Paulos 1980), rather than humour that is based on the social context of interactions. According to Paulos (1980: 11), 'both mathematics and humour are economical and explicit' and 'they are short and make sense without much context'. Given that individuals with Asperger syndrome are known to have problems in social interaction in which context is vital for understanding, they might also be lacking in their understanding of humour rooted in a social context. In one study participants were asked to choose one out of five possible funny joke endings (Emerich et al. 2003). The participants with Asperger syndrome did not understand the jokes in the way people without Asperger syndrome did. Instead of choosing the correct funny ending, they most frequently chose humorous but not coherent endings. Samson and Hegenloh (2010) analysed which cognitive or affective deficits caused problematic or decontextualized processing of jokes. The results of this study showed that individuals with Asperger syndrome had more difficulties than the control group in comprehending humorous material; they took the joking statement literally. This was supported by the fact that participants with Asperger syndrome commented on the jokes saying that a certain situation was 'not possible' or 'not realistic'. According to Samson and Hegenloh (2010), this is indicative of a problem with switching from a bona-fide reality-based mode to a non-bona-fide joke mode.

In sum, a lack of emotional intelligence, at least the trait aspects, seems to go hand in hand with the inability to appreciate humour in a social context. Not appreciating jokes seems to be part of the problems which people with Asperger syndrome encounter when interacting in a social context.

6 Emotional intelligence, health and negative emotions

Negative emotional experience and coping strategies

Many people agree that acknowledging and dealing effectively with emotions contributes to well-being, whereas ignoring or not dealing with emotions can have detrimental effects, especially if it is a prolonged or regular occurrence (e.g. Martins et al. 2010).

In contrast, the adaptive understanding and regulation of one's emotional states have positive implications for the health of body and mind (e.g. Schutte et al. 2007). Specifically, mental disorders where emotions play a central role, such as mood and anxiety disorders (e.g. Matthews et al. 2002), are related to emotional intelligence. People with higher levels of emotional intelligence may prevent negative emotional states becoming all pervasive by coping with the onset of these negative states more effectively than people with lower levels of emotional intelligence. In one study, in which negative mood was induced experimentally, participants with higher emotional intelligence were better able to repair their negative mood (e.g. Schutte et al. 2002). Additionally, people with higher EI perceive more satisfaction with social support, which, according to Schutte et al. (2007), might not only buffer physical illness, but also help the person to show better medical compliance and more commitment to health behaviour.

Constructs related to trait emotional intelligence are optimism and pessimism. Optimists compared with pessimists have a more positive outlook on life and score higher on EI abilities. A number of investigators have found that optimism and pessimism are important predictors of psychological well-being (e.g. Scheier et al. 2001). Higher scores on optimism are associated with better psychological adjustment, such as adjustment to stress (e.g. Chang et al. 1997). In contrast pessimism leads not only to lower ratings of life satisfaction but also to more stress and depression (e.g. Chang et al. 1997).

Deficits in emotion awareness as well as the inability to manage emotions are both symptoms identifying personality disorders (e.g. Matthews et al. 2002). In general higher EI is associated with better psychosocial functioning and reduced risk for psychosis (e.g. van Rijn et al. 2011), as well as enhanced optimism and interpersonal factors such as better social relationships (e.g. Schutte et al. 2001). In a meta-analysis Schutte et al. (2007) concluded their review by stating that higher EI is related to better health.

One theory suggests that depending on a person's current emotional state, they will react to emotional situations they encounter. The Emotion Context Insensitivity (ECI: Ellis et al. 2009) hypothesis predicts that a person in a negative mood state will be worse at reacting to and differentiating emotions they are faced with. In one experiment, Ellis et al. (2009) tested emotional reactivity of dysphoric and non-dysphoric individuals to positive and negative feedback about their performance on a task, which they were told would test their social intelligence. As expected, the results showed that depressed participants reported higher negative emotion and lower positive emotion compared with non-depressed controls before, during and after feedback. Furthermore, as the Emotion Context Insensitivity model predicted, although depressed people reported that they experienced higher negative emotions, they displayed fewer negative emotions behaviourally compared with controls when they received negative feedback. Additionally, the depressed participants did not differentiate their emotional reactions to positive and negative feedback, whereas the non-depressed group showed different emotions appropriate to the positive or negative context.

Although higher emotional intelligence has been found to relate to better mental health, in some cases higher intelligence might have negative effects (see Chapter 2), such that people high in EI are also more sensitive to mood induction and react more strongly to mood-related stimuli, which in the case of negative induction leads to stronger negative emotions and more distress (e.g. Petrides and Furnham 2003). Hence being high in EI is not always a protective factor.

Other people's negative emotions: how nurses or carers cope with negative emotions and violence in the workplace

Health care professionals are working in stressful situations, which frequently affect their mental and physical health. Research has found that psychiatric nurses feel stressed in their workplace (e.g. Ryan and

Quayle 1999). According to Gerits et al. (2005), violence and threats of violence are recognized problems among health care professionals, and nurses are commonly cited as the targets of such threats. So much so that one finds in many hospital Accident and Emergency wards, signs stating that physical or verbal violence against health care staff will not be tolerated. Being the target of challenging behaviours is a major factor predicting staff anxiety (Jenkins et al. 1997). Constant fear of threatening behaviour is a major stressor. However, not everybody reacts to stress in the same way, which recent work has attributed to EI.

Sarid et al. (2010) examined the effect of cognitive behavioural intervention (CBI) on stress perceptions of nurses and found that the group of nurses who underwent CBI felt less stressed and less fatigued compared to a control group who did not have the intervention. Given that CBI uses behavioural elements, namely relaxation and cognitive elements, which are designed to rebalance the perception of stressful events, this technique teaches skills which are part of EI (e.g. Bamber 2006). Sarid et al. (2010) concluded that by reducing physical and emotional stress as well as restructuring cognitively disturbing experiences into more positive perceptions, the CBI intervention helped to modify stress levels.

Among the many organizational stressors in hospital, there is one which has the highest stress rating, namely contact with death. The main consequences of stress which are either not acknowledged or not alleviated are alcoholism (e.g. McGrath et al. 2003), exhaustion and attempted suicides (e.g. Jones et al. 1987). In line with these findings, nurses show one of the lowest life expectancies of any profession (e.g. Jones et al. 1987), although it is not clear whether this is due to smoking, alcoholism or attempted suicide. However, as Sarid et al. (2010) noted, the effects of stress also depend on the type of personality and the ability of each person to handle and control emotions

Hunt and Evans (2004) investigated whether emotional intelligence can predict how individuals respond to traumatic experiences. They base their description of different methods of coping with traumatic stress on the description by Hunt and Robbins (1998), who interviewed war veterans. They found two main ways of coping: either people deal with traumatic events by talking about the events and by a method of narrative process transform the events so that over time memories of the trauma become easier to deal with. Others use avoidance techniques, such as avoiding situations which could potentially stir up memories of the trauma. Individuals who use avoidance tend not to process their traumatic memories, which may then return to their active memory at some point in the future. Processing information rather than avoidance is generally acknowledged to be a more effective coping strategy.

Emotions are evident in all aspects of nursing, which takes place in an environment which is emotionally charged and in which emotions are part of health care delivery (e.g. Bulmer-Smith et al. 2009). Emotions influence not only the nurses' professional relationships, but also their relationships at an intrapersonal level. This area of research brings together questions of the impact of emotions on individuals and their environment with the quest of researchers to identify what it means to use emotions constructively.

In one study relations between individual differences in susceptibility to emotional contagion and two self-reported emotion-related skills, namely how well people could identify emotions in others and regulate their own emotions, were examined (Papoušek et al. 2008). Films of women displaying sadness, happiness and neutral emotions were shown to female participants. Participants who could regulate their own emotions well but were less able to identify emotions in others were least affected by the sadness film. In contrast, the strongest responses to the film portraying positive affect were observed in those women who were weak at regulating their own emotions but reported good skills in emotion perception. These effects observed with subjective ratings of emotional contagion were replicated with cardiovascular measures of emotional arousal. According to Papoušek et al. (2008), these results indicate that the variance of susceptibility to emotional contagion can be explained by differences between people to sensitively perceive and regulate emotions.

In sum, research on EI, specifically those theories implicating both behavioural and cognitive aspects of emotion, concludes that EI ability on the whole facilitates decisions, helps to manage emotions, improves relationships, and ultimately results in better decisions (George 2000). Modern theories emphasize the functional nature of emotions. Yet, as Mikolajczak et al. (2008) point out, in addition to being a universal and recurring psychological process, emotion regulation is crucial for everyday life. Despite the importance of emotion regulation for adaptation, there is enormous variability in the ability and propensity of people to implement regulatory processes. Impaired emotional regulation can lead to critical consequences for social relationships and is detrimental to mental and physical health. However, sensitivity to affect is not always helpful, in that emotions can become dysfunctional when they are displayed at the wrong time, when they are of the wrong type, or when they are expressed with the wrong intensity (e.g. Gross and Thompson 2007). This is demonstrated by the fact that a majority of mental disorders involve some form of emotion dysregulation (Gross and Levenson 1997). Mikolajczak et al. (2008) observed that whereas some individuals chose to control their irritation when dealing with a problematic person, others lose their temper, and rather than finding a solution to a conflict, make the situation worse. It seems that a balanced view of emotions in which a person is sensitive to affect but is not overwhelmed by emotions, is the healthiest approach to work and personal life.

How such a balance might be achieved in the socialization of emotions from infancy to early childhood is the topic of the case study presented in the chapters which follow.

Part II
Case study

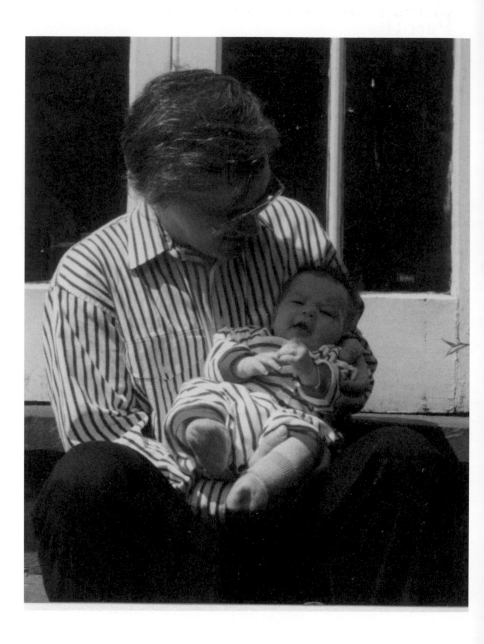

Introduction to the case study

The case study which follows was set in North London and Heidelberg, a university town in Germany. The main actors in this case study are a father and his daughter. The father, an American by birth, had lived and travelled all over the world, from Japan and Africa, where he studied, to India, Nepal and Belgium, where he worked for many years. The father, an Anthropologist, was the inspiration for the anthropological methods used in the analyses of the data collected by the mother a Psychologist. In this second part of the book, themes discussed in the first part of the book are re-examined. In this second part, fostering a concept of emotional intelligence is related to daily interactions between father and daughter as the baby starts to learn about emotions. Facilitating his daughter's emotional intelligence is discussed in various strands starting from the first few weeks of life. Development does not proceed uniformly. Rather in some areas we see more rapid development whereas others need more time. However, as we move through the development of the words used by her father to explain emotions to his daughter in Chapter 7, to when his daughter is talking to her father about emotions in Chapter 12, we can see the progress she has made in her first four years of life. The audiotaped conversation between father and daughter are transcribed and reported and then interpreted to give the reader a feel for the interactions as they unfold over time. These conversations reflect not only pride, joy and happiness, but also anger, frustration and sadness; they span the whole gamut of emotions all of us experience in daily life and which make for emotional development and specifically emotional intelligence in a social context.

7 The language of emotions from the first months of life

After coming back from the playground where Toto (16 months old) had fallen off the swings, her father remarks:

> We discovered, quite by accident, Newton's law of gravity, you know, that if you don't hold on to the swing any more, you fall to the ground.

In this first chapter of the case study we can see that the father communicates virtually from birth with his daughter about emotions. He tells her at 1 month of age that a smile is something he appreciates and that crying is to be discouraged. Parents in general and Toto's father in particular try to make sense of their children's emotional volatility from their earliest interactions, as the following example illustrates.

Toto is 2½ months old.

Father: Six forty three p. m. and we're trying to establish why you can be so miserable one moment and so happy the next. [Or a bit later] Yes, yes, you were going to explain to me that mystery of why it is you're so happy one moment and so sad the next.

An important part of socializing emotions includes parents talking to their children about these experiences (Eisenberg et al. 1998). Discussion of emotions, such as happiness, sadness, anger or fear, did occur when the Toto was in the middle of an emotional experience, or after the emotional experience had happened. Such discussions of emotions are assisting children in developing awareness of different emotional states and learning to recognize and label emotions (Denham et al. 1994).

As Toto matures, her father comments on the emotions she feels not only directly but also indirectly, as in the example when Toto (16 months old) falls off the swing:

Father: We discovered, quite by accident, Newton's law of gravity, you know, that if you don't hold on to the swing any more, you fall to the ground. If you'd made this discovery three hundred years ago you'd be famous.

The expressions of not only positive but also negative emotions are commented upon, for example concerning sadness:

Father: How does the sad Toto do it? How does Toto cry?
Toto: Aduh. Uh adur.

Her mother is more concerned and asks: 'Did you fall down there? Oh Toto. Poor Toto.'

Toto: Durur.
Mother: Did you cry a little bit?
Father: Well we had to give a bit of a cry, hey Toto?
Toto: (mumbling) Ur urur.

At 16 months her father also explains how the expression of anger manifests itself:

Father: How does Toto say give me that fast?
Toto: Ur ur.
Father: That's it. That's it.
Toto: Ur ur.
Father: Yeah. How does Toto say give me that one, at once otherwise I will be extremely angry?
Toto: Ahuh.
Father: Yea.

Children who understand their emotions and feel free to talk about their emotional experiences, that is children with more advanced emotional intelligence, are likely to be more skilled at controlling their own negative arousal (Eisenberg et al. 1998). However, in order to foster emotional intelligence, these discussions about emotions need to be embedded in warm parent–child relations (Denham et al. 1997) and they need to be instructive rather than controlling (Eisenberg et al. 1998).

Although Toto's father discusses sad or angry emotions, these negative emotions are much less talked about than happy emotions. According to Bloom (1998), language development occurs in a social context in that the words a child hears are related to the child's experience. Word learning is intimately connected to a child's emotional experience and it is via the emotions that the child learns the language to talk about them. Hence in the microcosm of the father talking to his daughter we can see that within the first four weeks of life, the baby is taught about what she likes and that her reactions to that liking are smiles. She is taught that there are situations she does not like and that her reactions to dislike are cries. The child's development of emotional understanding is illustrated in the context of Toto engaging with her father.

The melody of language, including the tone, inflection and pitch of our speech, teaches babies how to interpret daily events and inter-actions. For example, mothers use a higher pitch voice to express surprise when their babies do not show surprise during play than when the baby has learned that the situation is surprising (Reissland et al. 2002). Mothers also talk in a higher pitch when they interact with their babies in play compared with an ordinary situation (Reissland and Snow 1996), and they express information with varying pitch depend-ing on whether they are teaching their infant about positive or negative events in the environment (e.g. Fernald 1992).

Less is known about how the melody of language and the words we use teach children about emotions. In recent years, research on emotional learning has focused on parental socialization of children's feelings. Socialization takes place in day-to-day interactions between parents and their children, such as when a parent must handle a toddler's temper tantrum. Gottman and Declaire (1997) report one example in which a father manages to quieten his 2 year old's temper tantrum. The father, rather than getting annoyed at his daughter's public display of anger, expresses empathetic understanding of her frustration over a lost toy. In this case, his empathetic response helped the child cope with her negative emotions. The present case study will illustrate how parents and caregivers teach children about emotions through the use of language over time.

According to Zeidner et al. (2003), parents and caregivers support early language development by reinforcing what children say and by modelling how to speak. Subsequent learning is influenced by emo-tional discourse (the way in which individuals talk about emotions) with parents and others. Even though talking about emotions is important for emotional development, communication and especially social and emotional development begins at birth, long before children utter their first words (e.g. Cohen 2003). Hence infants start to learn about emotions before their parents can reinforce what infants say. Language development also occurs in a social context as the words a child hears are related to the child's experience (Bloom 1998). Word learning is intimately connected to a child's emotional experience and it is in the context of emotional experiences that the child learns the language to talk about these experiences.

Socialization of emotion during the first four months

Parents communicate with their babies from birth and they indicate at this early age already which emotions are to be encouraged and which ones are to be discouraged. Within the first months of life several emotions are distinguished for the baby.

The father communicating with his 1-month-old daughter tells her that a smile is something he appreciates. Whispering, the father says: 'A smile, are you going to give me a smile, a social smile? Smile.' Baby does not react and father says: 'Oh, no smiles?' Baby reacts and father approves, saying: 'OK I am much encouraged, I am much encouraged.'

In contrast, crying is to be discouraged as the father expresses dismay: 'Oh, oh, oh, what's this, eh? Nobody is going to believe you, when you tell them you cry when someone puts a shirt on. We'll just stay clear of a cry-baby or something.'

The father also validates his daughter's emotion expressions, as in the following example, a few days later, in which he anticipates his daughter's protest: 'I think I'll try putting this shirt back on you. This is the one where you cry every time I put it on. I don't know why, do you? You don't know why either. Hmm, OK, so now for the big moment . . . (Softly) Heh?'

Once the daughter is crying he tries to lighten the mood. Interrupting her crying he says: 'You're contesting it in court are you?' As his daughter's cries get more intense, he says: 'Ohh oh!? But I thought I was the boss!?' He acknowledges her protest: 'You really don't like that.'

While she continues crying, he continues dressing her. He tries to stop her crying, saying: 'Hey, come on now! Where does that crying come from?' Later her father suggests that she must have learned to cry when being dressed and he speculates: 'If everything's imitation

. . . now I don't cry like that, (I wonder) where have you learnt that from?'

Once Toto no longer cries, her father makes her crying the topic of conversation: 'Where have you learnt that from?' He then points out to Toto:

> You have your own bed; you have our bed, a constant food source. Yeah, nobody'll believe you if you cry. When they say: 'What're you crying about?' You'll say, 'Well, I have two beds, constant food source . . .' 'Hmm?' '. . . colourful clothes . . .' 'Hmm?' '. . . two goofy doting parents . . .' And everybody will say: 'What?! And you're complaining?! Yeah, nobody'll believe you.'

Praising and reinforcing desirable emotions during the first four months

In addition to being taught that likes are associated with smiles and dislikes with cries, Toto is also taught more complex social rules in the first few months, namely about polite behaviour.

When Toto is 12 weeks old, her father talks about a party they attended:

Father:	Five thirty p.m. Post mortem on a party.
Toto:	Eh
Father:	What was your reaction? What was your reaction? Did you like the food?
Toto:	Ah! Ahaa ah.
Father:	Yeah, that milk huh? It wasn't so bad, huh? And the guests – did you like the guests?
Toto:	Eh.
Father:	No, not so interesting.
Toto:	Eh! Ah ah.
Father:	What about the host and hostess?
Toto:	Aha aaaaah!
Father:	Yeah! Uncle Jim and Auntie Ann!
Toto:	Aaah!
Father:	Yea, they're very nice.
Toto:	Ha! Ha! Ha! Oh.
Father:	Yeah; and did you enjoy yourself?
Toto:	Aha! Aaah! Aaah!
Father:	Yeah you had a good time. Well that's nice.

Toto:	Ah haa!
Father:	Well that's really nice.
Toto:	Heheh! Ahh! Hehh!
Father:	Did you think so as well? Yeah, I think so. Hmm? Yes?
Toto:	Hah! Aaaah! Ah!
Father:	You didn't cry at all and you were very polite!

A few days later, her father praises her not only for coping with separation but also for seemingly enjoying it.

Father:	So. You had an active morning?
Toto:	Ah aaaaaah!
Father:	Oh! Yes. Did you enjoy this morning? Hmm? Do you realize that this morning you were separated from us for the first time?
Toto:	Ooh ah!
Father:	Yes! So you enjoyed it? Yeah.
Toto:	Ooh, eh.
Father:	Yeah, and it was the first time you were separated away from us. The midwife had you. For fifteen minutes!
Toto:	Wehh! Ahaaaa. Ahaa!
Father:	Yeah. Yeah. You coped admirably. Hmm. Yeah.
Toto:	Haaa. Aaah.
Father:	We had the impression that you didn't miss us at all! Did you know that? Yeah. You were enjoying yourself, mm?
Toto:	Aah!
Father:	Yeah.

The father's praise is effective. After 4 months Toto no longer cries as much when being dressed as the following excerpt shows:

Father:	Do you have any idea how this works? Hmm? Perhaps, if we unbutton this first . . . This is more difficult than meets the eye! Yah, this – the zipper, made in Britain, is like the toilet chains on British toilets. Hmm? It takes a lot of local knowledge of just how much to pull and what sort of twist to give, to get the thing to flush. It doesn't want to zip!
Toto:	Ha haoo!
Father:	Oh you're delighted are you? Let's try this one again. I'm going to have to give up!
Toto	(hic-cups)
Father:	Yeah! And you're tickled pink! I'm going to have to give up!

Talking about fear and using humour in the fifth month

Around Toto's fifth month, her father introduces fear into her vocabulary:

Father: What did you think of the clinic? Hm? Yeah. It was really nothing huh?
Toto: Ah.
Father: Yes. It was really nothing; nothing to worry about.
Toto: Eh, eh!
Father: You're ready for your next injection are you?
Toto: Ha.
Father: Just give the date and the place. You'll show up, hmm? Nothing to fear!
Father: Yeah. We're testing the vocal cords.
Toto: Waaaaaaaahhhh!!!!!
Father: One, two.
Toto: Wwaaaauaahhh! Waaaha-ahhhh!
Father: Testing one, two, three, four. Can you read me? Vocal cord testing time!
Toto: Waaaaaaaaaah!
Father: Yeah. Yeah. I think they can hear you outside as well as inside. Yeah. I think they can hear you. No problem there. Hmm. You don't need a loudspeaker, I don't think.
Toto: Waaaaaalililili!
Father: Yeah. Yeah, if there's anything that, you know, bothers you or something and you want some service, mm? I think your vocal cords will be loud enough, to get the message to the end of the house mm? We don't need an alarm bell or a service bell – a buzzer. No. I think the passage of air past the old epiglottis, combined with a few sort of throat and tongue movements, mm? Yeah. The signal is loud and clear. Mm. I think so. Yeah.

This type of talk continues for a while and then the father records later in the month:

Father: Yes. So you've stopped crying a bit now, mm? You've stopped crying. Yeah. Why were you crying in the first place?
Toto: Ha!

Father:	Why, that was the reason! Yeah, you were trying to stretch your lungs. To see how many decibels you could record. Yeah, it's a pity we don't have a decibel index on the tape recorder. Would that be nice? Would it? Then we could compare you with our neighbours, mm? And we could record you and play it up at the maximum volume.
Toto:	Heh.
Father:	Mm, and retaliate.
Toto:	Aaah ooh hoo!
Father:	Through the thin walls!

Also bedtime is still a difficult time at this age and crying still continuous. Again the father uses humour when trying to get his daughter into bed at night-time and when trying to get her out of bed in the mornings.

Father:	So it's the evening.
Toto:	Wuh ah!
Father:	Ten to nine.
Toto:	Ha!
Father:	We're hypothesizing that you're tired and you want to go to bed. All you want is a little nappy change, just a little nappy change, and then you go straight to bed. Pleased as punch, yeah.
Toto:	Uwuh.
Father:	Yes, that's how we've interpreted your cries and grunts over the last half hour.
Toto:	Ah!
Father:	You're saying please put me to bed after you've changed my nappy. I'm a bit tired, I feel like going to sleep. OK. Here comes the moment, hm? I am picking you up. I am carrying you over to the cot, I give you a little kiss, another little kiss, and I lower you down into the bed. I pull the quilt over you. You can't believe what's happening to you. You think there must be some mistake.
Toto:	Waaaaaah!.
Father:	You're moving your legs, you are trying to escape! Hm?
Toto:	A, A, Hoo.
Father:	Night-night. Night-night, Toto.
Toto:	Ah!
Father:	Night-night. OK?
Toto:	Ah. Ah-ah!Ah! Ah!

Father: OK. I suppose I must have misunderstood you. I must have misunderstood you. Shall we go downstairs? I'll turn this off, mm? You win.

The next morning, however:

Father: Toto! Wake up!

Toto (cries).

Father: Toto! You're a hundred days old today, mm? A hundred days old. It's your hundredth birthday. Yeah! It's your hundredth birthday. Today is the ninth of August, Toto waking up at the adolescent hour of nine-fifty, on her one hundredth birthday. Rather, she is being woken up on her one hundredth birthday. And she doesn't like it.

Toto (cries).

Father: Be a lion! A monkey?? Come on now, do your little call!

Toto: Ha.

Father: Come on.

Toto: Awuh!

Father: That's it. What a loud call!

Toto: Aaaargh! Waaaah! Waah! Aaaarggh! Aaah! Ah!

Father: Yeah! What a roar!

Toto: Aaaaaaaaah!

Father: What a roar!

Toto: Aaaaaaah! Aaaah!

Father (laughing): Yeah. Fantastic!

Toto: Aoooo! Waaaaah!

Father: Fantastic! For your hundredth birthday!

Toto: Ahem, ahem.

Father: Oh! It makes you have a sore throat that roar doesn't it? What a roar!

Toto: Waaaaaah!

Father: This roar is now a grunt! It's becoming a grunt isn't it?

Toto: Ah, ah!

Father: Yeah. Yeah. Call of the wild! The call of the wild. Oh! You really put your vocal cords to the test!

Toto: Waaaah! Waaaaaargh! Waaah!

Father: Oh – OK OK OK, yes enough of this.

Learning to talk about objects from 6 months onwards

Until around 6 months of age, the father talks many times about emotions, identifying them and relating them to positive or negative events. However, after that time the tape recordings reveal very little reference to emotions. During this second half of the first year and well into the second year, the father only occasionally talks about emotions. He is more concerned with the fact that she does not sleep and what words she might express.

At this time the father teaches her a vocabulary such as when Toto is 1 year old and they are reading a picture book, *Babar the Elephant*.

Toto: Bu, bu, bu.
Father: Babar, OK? Travelling up in their balloon and look way down there, that's the planet earth. What do you see?
Toto: Wow, wow.
Father: There's a wow, wow (dog) and what's this?
Toto: Brum, brum.
Father: What else do you call that? Do you have another word maybe, a bit more adult like?
Toto: Ho ho!
Father: Yea, if you don't mind we can shift from verbal icons to symbols, Toto. Wouldn't you call that a car?
Toto: Wow, wow.

Another example of learning occurs in the context of playing with blocks when Toto is 20 months old:

Father: Get me the yellow one. Can you get Daddy the yellow block?
Toto: Daa.
Father: That's green, that's blue, that's yellow.
Toto: Blue.
Father: That's blue, yea. OK, can you give Daddy the red one? Where's the red one?
Toto: Daa.
Father: That's yellow, which one is red?

Her father also talks about remembered events:

Father: Where were you yesterday? Did you go to a farm house?
Toto: Yea.
Father: Did you see a cow?
Toto: Yes.
Father: Did you see any pigs?
Toto: Yea.

Father: Did you see any kitty cats?
Toto: An doggy.
Father: And doggies as well? What did the doggy do?
Toto: Ai ai.
Father: You did 'ai ai' (stroke) to the doggy?

Research has shown that as the child is perceived by the parent to understand more, language becomes simplified. Development proceeds in a so-called U-curve, so that at a very early age, language to the baby is quite complex and becomes simpler as the baby grows older. Sherrod et al. (1977) reported that maternal utterances to younger pre-linguistic children are more complex as measured by the mean length of the utterance (MLU) used than those to older pre-linguistic children. This difference in complexity of speech addressed to infants might be based on the ability of younger pre-linguistic – in comparison with older pre-linguistic – children's ability to process language input. Differences in the complexity of child-directed speech might be driven by infants' reactions to verbal input. However, in one study (Reissland et al. 1999), differences of maternal child-directed speech were unrelated to the frequency of infant vocalizations, but rather seemed to depend on maternal perception of their infant's maturity. In that study, although premature and term infants vocalized approximately the same amount, mothers of premature infants, compared with mothers of term infants, asked more complex questions. This change in perception of what the baby understands seems to lead to a change in emphasis in socialization.

Learning to talk about emotions in the second year

Once Toto speaks a few words, emotion socialization changes dramatically. Toto can answer questions about emotions and she can also signal her happiness by a laugh, which she knows is the appropriate response. Hence Toto (22 months) answers with an emotional reaction when her father asks her what she is going to do at the babysitter's house:

Father: We have to go to Marget's this morning don't we? What's
             Toto going to do at Marget's?
Toto: Laow.
Father: Laugh? Oh that's nice. I'd really be happy if you were to
             laugh a bit.

One month later, her father asks: 'Did she say she was happy to see you? Yeah?'

Toto: Yeah.
Father: Well, I thought she would be.

At this age Toto also learns to understand that others, especially her mother, worry about her when she does certain things and that she can control the emotional reactions of others by refraining from doing them. The father reinforces this knowledge by asking her questions:

Father: What's that? Oh, is that your lip cream.
Toto: Top.
Father: Where is the top?
Toto: Mouth.
Father: Yeah, it's not supposed to go in the mouth is it? That's what Mummy said, didn't she?
Toto: No. No.
Father: Yeah exactly, Mummy said no, no.
Toto: Have in.
Father: You have it. I know you wanted to have it, but you're not supposed to play with it that way.
Toto: Flow.
Father: Yeah, oh. Yeah. Oh, that's nice. That's a clever little thing.
Toto: Bow.
Father: Yeah, what did Mummy say?
Toto: No.
Father: Exactly, and why did Mummy say no?
Toto: A play.
Father: Yeah, you play. Mummy was worried, wasn't she? You shouldn't be putting it into your mouth, uh? Is that what Mummy said? Let's see if we can find the lid, it must be in your handbag. Here it is.
Toto: Mouth?
Father: Not in your mouth. Mummy gets very, very upset.
Toto: Mouth? In a mouth?
Father: In the mouth? No I don't think so.
Toto: Mouth?
Father: No.

On another occasion, the father asks: 'You don't want Mummy to worry about you?'

Toto: No.

Yet another time the father reinforces the same message: 'Exactly, but Mummy says no, no.'

Toto: In nur mouth.
Father: Not in the mouth.
Toto: Yeah.
Father: Then Mummy gets very, very upset doesn't she? Very worried.

Conclusion

The communication between the father and daughter described in this chapter demonstrates how parents foster emotional development through the words they speak with their children. In the context of daily conversations, babies learn which emotions are desirable or undesirable and ultimately how to control their expression of emotions. This study further demonstrates how, for the first six months of life, parents spend a great deal of time communicating with their infants about these emotions. However, during the second half of the first year and well into the second year, parental dialogue consisted of simpler language and emphasized learning vocabulary and behavioural rules. This developmental progression from talk revolving around the infant's feelings, to talk that increasingly focusses not only the child's vocabulary but also her cognitive skills, suggests that in infancy children first learn about emotions during interactions in which feeling the emotion is emphasized. Later, they learn the vocabulary to talk about these emotions and how to manage them effectively. Parents and other caregivers support their children's healthy emotional development through the sensitive use of language during daily interactions and activities.

This chapter illustrates the labelling of emotions and teaching about emotions in a social context. We can follow the process from the first few weeks of life to when Toto asserts her independence as a toddler. As she matures so her father gives her more responsibilities for her actions and her moral obligations towards others. Even as a 2 year old, she learns that she needs to behave in such a way that others do not get hurt.

Although only the American father's communication with his daughter is presented here, we have to remember that learning occurs in a cultural as well as social context. In a study by Wang (2001), American and Chinese mothers were asked to discuss with their 3 year olds events during which the children experienced happiness, sadness, fear or anger. American mother–child conversations showed an 'emotion-explaining style' in which mothers and children provided rich causal explanations for antecedents of emotions. Chinese mother–child conversations employed an 'emotion-criticizing style' that focused on installing proper behaviour in the child and gave few explanations for the emotion itself. American mother–child conversations also tended to centre on personal themes and were more focused on the child's roles and predilections than the conversations of Chinese mothers and infants.

The importance of taking socialization practices into account when applying findings was pointed out by Kennedy-Moore and Watson (1999), who argued that emotional expression can on the one hand help people to label and understand their emotions. It helps to extract information from them, and in that way it fosters emotional insight, directs coping efforts, and should lead to enhanced well-being. On the other hand, emotional expression may be harmful when expression is not related to insight; it is either at the lowest levels of emotional awareness, or disguises genuine feelings. In these cases, emotional expression may be harmful because it merely intensifies negative feelings and interferes with functioning.

In sum, the developmental case study presented here applies to educated middle-class parents and might not apply to other social or cultural groups. Nevertheless it gives an insight into the process of how babies learn about emotionally intelligent behaviour by interacting with their parents.

8   Acoustic aspects of emotion talk

Father waking Toto up from her sleep:

> Somebody has disturbed my sleep. The great sleep of Toto. They
> will be punished. I will roar. I will grumble.

The influence of sound on the appraisal of emotion

The abilities to perceive and express emotion are together considered
to be the most basic component of emotional intelligence. Although
basic, this aspect of EI is nonetheless extremely complex, and includes
the ability to register, attend to and decipher emotional messages.
Discussions concerning basic components of EI are mostly focused on
speech-based communication; nevertheless the topic can be addressed
as a more general problem, in that vocal EI components include both
the use of acoustics to influence others and the production of functional responses to such sounds. According to the 'affect-induction
framework' of Bachorowski and Owren (2002), sound influences
inherently a listener's emotional system. A hearer listening to a sound
will appraise the significance of that sound. This appraisal of the
meaning of the sound plays an important mediating role. Evaluating a
sound to indicate happiness, for example, will help the individual
to respond appropriately to the message conveyed through sound.
According to the affect-induction framework, sound is a means by
which a signaller can modulate the behaviour of a listener. Through
sound, a person can influence attention, arousal and the emotional
states of a listener. This implies that although vocal signals do not
carry symbolic information in the same way as words, they still
influence the listener in the way he or she interprets the sound.
Specifically, the effect of the emotional message carried in the nonverbal channel is based on a combination of an impact on the

emotions of a listener as well as the impact the sound has on the appraisal processes of a listener when hearing the emotional message. A speaker of an emotional message influences a listener directly, by the effect of the acoustic emotional expression as well as indirectly, by learned emotional responses resulting from previous pairings of an individual's sounds with subsequent affect-inducing events.

Positive and negative emotion talk has been analysed in terms of differences in pitch over time and the affective valence of the talk. The pitch of emotional communication does influence the child's development. Pitch of voice has been found to be an important aspect in socialization since before they can understand the spoken words infants attend to the pitch in which the message is voiced. In the case of maternal depression, for example, the pitch of the depressed mother's voice changes depending on whether she talks to her infant or reads a picture book. Depressed mothers read the text of a picture book with a significantly lower pitch of voice than non-depressed mothers. Non-depressed mothers read the text of a picture book in a pitch which is similar to the high voiced pitch used when they talk 'motherese' to the baby. In contrast, depressed mothers use an even higher pitch of voice compared with the pitch of non-depressed mothers talking to their baby. Since pitch of voice carries maternal emotions, this higher pitch of voice used when talking to the baby might express the stress these mothers are under when interacting with their baby in front of an audience (Reissland et al. 2003).

The meaning of the message is carried by sound

It is widely acknowledged that pitch of voice carries the meaning of the message. One consistently reported feature of child directed speech is that parents use a high frequency of questions (Snow 1977). when speaking to their infants, ranging from 25 to 60 per cent of the utterances sampled (Stern et al. 1982; Sullivan and Horowitz 1983). Parents differentiate types of questions with differing pitch of voice, namely, they distinguish between questions which require their children to take their turn in the conversation and questions which do not require an answer nor give leave for the child to speak. Questions fulfil various functions. At the simplest level, when interpreted directly, the utterance of a question is a request for information. Although questions addressed to young infants are in one sense always rhetorical because the infant cannot respond, one can still differentiate between those questions which, if addressed to an older child or adult, might be called 'real' and those which might be called 'rhetorical'. Green (1989: 154–155) argued that one can distinguish 'sincere questions', which indicate that the speaker wants some information which the addressee is believed to have, from 'rhetorical questions', in which the speaker either assumes everyone knows or no one knows the answer. According to Green (1989), there is, however, another level at which one can analyse the functions that questions have in conversations, namely that of indicating when there is a switch of roles from speaker to addressee and vice versa. A question will usually indicate a switch of roles (Schlegloff 1979), 'although by definition, rhetorical questions so understood will not do this' (Green 1989: 153). When the child understands the real question he or she is potentially capable of answering it with a word or specific babbling (e.g. Waterson 1978; Blake and Fink 1987).

The pitch of voice of Toto's father distinguished emotional connotations of 'real' and 'rhetorical' questions. Real questions were those to which the father wanted the child to give him information, such as 'Do you want red socks?' An example of a real question at 1 month in the context of getting dressed was: 'So we want to put a T-shirt underneath. The yellow one. Do you like that?' or in the context of getting ready to feed her: 'Are you hungry?'

At 5 months a real question was: 'Is it tasty?' and at 15 months: 'Do you want to come down?' (from the changing table after having dressed her, rather than stay and read a book).

Rhetorical questions, in contrast, are questions that the speaker never intended to be answered. They are used to make a point rather than to get information. For example a rhetorical question at 1 month was asked in the following context of changing the nappy: 'A bit cool. One giant sized nappy . . . of containing it all. I need three hands. Can I borrow one of yours?'

Or in the context of having to get ready to meet her uncle: 'And we've got to walk there (the station). You can't even crawl yet, let alone walk. Do you think you're going to make it?'

An example of a rhetorical question at 5 months is: 'Mrs B. has gone but she'll be back in seven hours. Are we going to manage that?' and at 15 months is: 'Shall we turn off the Watergate tape?' when Toto is dressed and ready to go out.

The results showed that there was a significant difference between the mean pitch for real (mean = 138 Hz) and rhetorical (mean = 168 Hz) questions at 15 months and that this significant difference persisted at 16 months (real questions: mean = 144 Hz; rhetorical questions: mean = 168 Hz), but was absent at earlier ages. The results showed that from the time the child was 15 months old, her father differentiated real from rhetorical yes–no questions by speaking in a significantly higher mean pitch when asking rhetorical questions compared to the mean pitch when asking real questions. When asking real questions at 1, 5, 10, 15 and 16 months, the mean fundamental frequency of paternal speech was 143 Hz, which is similar to that recorded by other researchers (e.g. Siegel et al. 1990) with regard to a global measure of paternal infant-directed language. They found that the mean fundamental frequency of paternal speech to infants was 154 Hz and their mean fundamental frequency to adults was 121 Hz. Specifically, Warren-Leubecker and Bohannon (1984) found that declaratives were spoken by fathers with a mean pitch of 150 Hz and questions with a mean of 156 Hz to 2-year-old children. The mean pitch of father's speech to adults was 114 Hz.

By the time the child was 15 months old, the father used a higher mean fundamental frequency than at 10 months and younger, in order to differentiate rhetorical questions (mean = 167 Hz) from real questions (mean = 140 Hz). It is around this age that infants start to map certain babbling sounds onto specific meanings (Blake and Fink 1987). Furthermore, at around 15–16 months of age, children start to answer yes–no questions such as 'Do you want some more?' with 'More,' or 'Do you want to get down?' with 'Down' (Tomasello 1992). Although children at 10 months or younger might understand certain questions, it is only at the time when children start to use language by either using specific babbling sounds or specific words, that in the present study the father distinguished real from rhetorical questions through their pitch height.

Furthermore, it is at that time that questions are used by parents as tutorial devices (Snow et al. 1976), as requests for actions (Newport et al. 1977), or as requests for clarification (Cherry 1976).

At the age of 16 months, although the father distinguishes between real and rhetorical questions, and as is shown in the following extract even when asking 'real' questions, he still directs Toto's actions:

Toto   (babbles): Dadado oh oh.
Father: That's a book. Toto, Toto.
Toto: Oh eeunim.
Father: Do you want to read? Do you want to read a book?
Toto: Oh lur.
Father: Yeah, you pick one. You take one down.
Toto: Urururururur.
Father: Let's see what do we have here to read?

Toto:	Ohbe uh adeeda.
Father:	That one?
Toto:	Adedur.
Father:	Oh that's one of the more boring little ones. Here's one, here's a nice one. Shall we read this one?
Toto:	Ururur.
Father:	Um.

Not only does the father distinguish between real and rhetorical questions but also he distinguishes between 'real' and 'pretend' emotions as expressed by his daughter. This is exemplified in the following exchange about her third vaccination when she is 16 months old:

Father:	It is now the first of September. Time for Toto to get dressed. So this morning Toto you are going to get a little injection. OK, it will just be like a little bee, it'll go buzzz, ping, just like that. Buzzz, ping and it will be all over, nothing more than that.
Toto:	Urdunur.
Father:	It's true, yeah. The first time you had an injection Toto, the first time you didn't cry at all.
Toto:	Ah brrumbrrrumbrrrrrum.
Father:	You took it like a man. We were so proud.
Toto:	Barrrup.
Father:	Yeah. You were only a few weeks old. A little baby no bigger than, no bigger than that. And you didn't cry at all, you didn't flinch. Um. Didn't even blink.
Toto:	Umaaraararrrr.
Father	(laughing): A stiff upper lip there was. Um.
Toto:	Brrum brrrumm.
Father	(imitating Toto): Brrum brrrumm. Second time we went for an injection.
Toto	(starts to cry).
Father:	That's how you were exactly.
Toto	(blows raspberries): Burrrr.
Father:	That's how you were exactly. You became immediately suspicious. Um? Didn't you? You said what are they doing there? Huh? Even before the doctor got the needle out you were crying.
Toto:	Bahbom.
Father:	And then we were wrestling. Yeah. We were all wrestling.

Toto: Orororororororor.
Father: Trying to pin you down.
Toto: Burwah.
Father: But this time I'm certain you'll be very, very sweet. I'm certain you'll be very, very sweet this time.
Toto   (starts to cry).
Father: Because you're so much older and mature. Um? You don't cry any more do you Toto?
Toto   (cries).
Father: You play at crying a lot though don't you? Um? To keep us on our toes.
Toto: Ururur.
Father: I know you. You pretend to be in great agony.
Toto   (blowing raspberries).
Father: Yeah.

In summary, only at the older age of 15 months did the father distinguish questions which should be answered from questions which should not be answered. Hence, although at the younger age one could argue that all questions are rhetorical because the infant cannot answer any, or conversely that all questions are real because parents behave as if children do understand all questions (e.g. Kaye 1982), in the present study, the father did only distinguish in his pitch between real and rhetorical questions when his daughter was 15 months old. Hence, it is suggested that by 15 months, not only do parents take into account the child's ability to understand what is said by modifying their infant-directed speech (e.g. Ferrier 1978), but also more specifically, the father in the present study varied the pitch in which he asked the questions. At this age rhetorical questions are asked more playfully, indicated by the higher pitch. Given that a question will usually indicate a switch of roles (Schlegloff 1979), one function of the difference in pitch between real and rhetorical questions at 15 months, might be to indicate turns or non-turns in conversations.

Infant-directed language has been analysed with special attention to the prosodic forms that often express the pragmatic or social inter-actional functions (Snow and Goldfield 1983; Fernald and Kuhl 1987; Papoušek 1992; Reissland and Snow 1996). For example, Papoušek (1992) suggested that prosody can signal 'rewarding', 'discouraging' and 'soothing' contexts, and that the pitch contour is an especially salient aspect of caregivers' speech that supports the child's concep-tualization of these social meanings in the first months of life. Given that the baby is too young to understand explanations, this is one way of indicating to the baby which emotions are real and have to be taken seriously, and which are pretend or not as important and can be ignored. In sum, many studies have confirmed the claim that pitch is the most important aspect of prosody that parents use to mark different pragmatic and social situations. Fernald and Kuhl (1987) found that fundamental frequency, rather than timing or amplitude, was the aspect of child-directed speech that 4-month-old children responded to differentially. Accordingly, pitch is the variable most often identified in vocalizations by infants (e.g. D'Odorico and France 1991) and by adults (e.g. Warren-Leubecker and Bohannon 1984; Fernald et al. 1989; Cooper et al. 1997;). In effect, it seems that babies and adults rely on the melody of the message and young children who understand and can talk rely on the content of speech. For example, Morton and Trehub (2001) tested children and adults, who heard forty utterances, spoken by a female speaker. Sentences with happy or sad content were recorded twice, once with a happy para-language and once with a sad para-language. Children and adults were asked to listen to the female speaker and say whether the speaker was happy or sad. The results showed that adults relied exclusively on para-language, that is the pitch of voice in which the sentence was spoken, in order to identify the 'real' emotion of the speaker. In contrast, 4 year olds responded primarily to the content of the utterance and would claim that a speaker saying 'I am happy' in a sad voice, would still be happy. Hence, babies, having no words, and adults, understanding words and the intention of the message, behave similarly by relying on para-language. In contrast children at the beginnings of lexical understanding take the words they hear to be the meaning of the message.

In summary, the pitch of speech directed to a baby is seen as especially important for the child to understand what is being communicated, not only semantically but also in terms of their roles in conversational exchanges.

Questions about feelings and questions about thoughts

Emotional intelligence is fostered not only by talking about emotions but also by indicating how to cope with emotions. The following analysis concentrated on types of questions asked in the context of emotionally charged situations. The diary entries were searched for questions asking about the child's feelings in general (e.g. 'What do you feel?') and compared to questions asking about the child's thoughts (e.g. 'What do you think?').

Given that the father uses a different pitch to distinguish between real and rhetorical questions starting from 15 months of age, in what situations does the father ask about feelings and when does he ask about thoughts?

Toto's father asked her about her opinions and thoughts from the first recordings. Questions about Toto's thoughts are usually rhetorical, such as when she is 3 months old:

Father: OK, come on now, tell me a bit more, what's on your mind? You met the dentist? What did you think of him? Mr Gavin?
Toto: Ah. Huh hah!
Father   (translating): Hmm? Nice guy?

In August, when she is 4 months old, her father asks:

So what do you think of the summer, hmm? What do you think of the summer? Hm? Yeah. This is your first English summer. Yeah. It's a good thing you weren't asleep or you might have missed it. It's a good thing you've been awake, otherwise you might have missed it. Yeah. Yeah.

There are many examples of asking Toto about her thoughts throughout the recordings. In contrast, questions about feelings start only when she has reached around 6 months of age and are rare in the recordings.

The father asks when she is 6 months and 12 days old:

How do you feel this morning, Toto?

The next time her father asks about her feelings is when she has reached 8 months of age and he asked her the same question, namely:

How are you feeling today?

When she reaches 1 year of age, her father asks:

How does it feel to be clean?

When she is 13 months old her father, in the context of her being naughty by eating dirt off the floor, refers to Toto's feelings saying:

Toto, you shouldn't do that. It's not good for you. Does it feel funny? I hope it does. Hope, it's harmless. We try to feed you such good things to eat and you don't take them.

Toto replies, 'Babaa' (babytalk for meaning dirty).

Finally, when she has reached 15 months, her father asks when she cries:

Oh Toto, are you really feeling so fragile this evening?

In sum, talking about feelings, both physical and emotional, in general in contrast to talking about thoughts in general occurs very rarely at this age. Rather the father, as I showed in Chapter 7, talks about specific emotion indicators, such as a 'smile' or a 'cry'. This is followed by using labels for happiness, sadness, fear or anger during specific emotional events. In contrast, the father mentions 'feelings' as abstract concepts, only in passing at this early stage of development. The next chapter examines the father's rhetorical use of language and illustrates the development of the father's perception of the increased sophistication of his daughter and how her ability and willingness to comply with requests, such as not to eat dirt from the floor, changes over time.

9 On the changing table

The use of rhetoric with an infant

Toto, 5 months 23 days old, cries.

Father:　One second, here's your song Toto. 'I just want to warn you if our paths should cross, my name is Toto and I'm the boss.'

The mutual influence of parent and infant

Long before children can speak, adults perceive infant vocalizations to have different meanings. They interpret cooing sounds as more communicative than other, less speech-like, infant sounds (Beaumont and Bloom 1993). Hence, an infant's increasing cooing or vocalizing results in more active engagement with adults (Lavelli and Fogel 2005). Particularly in the early years, affective interactions in everyday experiences with others influence understanding of information about ourselves and others (e.g. Malatesta 1990) and lead to the ability to perceive, understand and manage emotions (Salovey and Mayer 1990) and behaviour (Bruner 1982). According to Brackett et al. (2004), higher emotional intelligence is related to positive outcomes such as pro-social behaviour, parental warmth, and positive peer and family relations. The question of the differentiation of ego from alter in the context of emotional development is unclear. The change of focus from the baby's own emotions to the baby's ability to incorporate other's emotions is the topic of the present study. In what follows I report and analyse an everyday encounter which caused some friction, namely getting dressed, in order to follow Toto's emotional development in terms of how she made sense of her own emotions vis-à-vis her father's expression of emotions. According to Fogel et al. (2002), the infant's intrapersonal self-dialogues are intertwined with interpersonal dialogues from the first days of life. Consequently, modern research on infancy tends to reject the notion of an 'autistic' or 'individual' sense of self in early infancy, as postulated in some early versions of psychoanalytic theory (e.g. Stern 1985).

From the first months of life there is an increase in mutual influence between an infant and the caregiver's behaviour (Lavelli and Fogel 2005). The infant's enhanced ability to engage and reciprocate in dyadic interaction alters how parent and child interact in terms of not only quantitative changes, such as increased vocal input by the child, but also the qualitative changes in caregiver–infant interaction. This dialogical process can be understood in terms of regularly recurring routines or frames, which are defined as either rigid and unchanging or creative and changing behavioural interactions. Fogel et al. (2002) analysed these frames in a case study of one child and her mother's behavioural interactions during three periods, namely, 0–6 months, 6–12 months and 12–18 months.

This mutual influence of parent and infant is manifested not only behaviourally but also verbally. Basic to development is the child's ability to distinguish the self 'I' from the other 'You', as it allows the child to make sense of his or her emotions vis-à-vis the other's emotions. In the negotiation of meaning that is always present between the person issuing a message and the person receiving the message, one of the key elements is the reference of personal pronouns. The first and second person pronouns are especially important for communication because of the implications they have for both participants in the speech event. Among the pronouns that refer to elements of the environment, it is assumed that 'I' and 'we' represent the speaker or writer, and 'you' the addressee (hearer or reader). However, the referent of these pronouns is not always so clear. As Biber et al. (1999: 329) point out, 'the meaning of the first person plural is often vague' or 'the second person "you" is similar to "we" in being used with different intended referents'. This vagueness has led these authors to state that it is usually left to the addressee to infer who is included in the reference. According to Fortanet (2004), the use of these personal pronouns is an important indicator of how audiences are conceptualized by speakers. She argued that the use of 'I', 'you' and 'we' is especially marked as a rhetorical indicator, which clarifies the level of attempted rapport and involvement of the speaker with the audience. Fortanet (2004) analysed the inclusive and exclusive use of 'we'. Using 'we' inclusively is a rhetorical device which establishes a common concern, interest or responsibility, whereas when 'we' is used exclusively, it distances the speaker from the audience. Relating the choice of pronouns to the intended creation of distance between the speaker and the receiver of the message, Kamio (2001) highlights the gradation of closeness from 'we', which is psychologically the closest through 'you' to 'they', which he considers as 'psychologically very distant' (Kamio 2001: 1120–1121).

Research indicates that in speech to babies and young children, parents use 'you' most frequently followed by 'I' followed by 'we' (Laakso and Smith 2004). Mirroring child-directed speech, the use of 'we' in the child's own language occurs relatively late compared to 'I' or 'you'. Nelson (1975) found when analysing spontaneous speech of twenty-four 2 year olds, that only five of the twenty-four children used 'we' a total of seven times. Hence, only very few children said 'we' and those who uttered 'we' did so only very infrequently. Chil dren, however, do understand that when they are addressed as 'you' it means that the 'I' is requested to respond. This becomes clear when one analyses the use of 'I', 'you' and 'we' in a corpus of child language, where, according to Nelson's (1975) findings, the use of 'I' (231 times) is much more prevalent than the use of 'you' (45 times) or 'we' (7 times).

In the first few months of life, infant vocal behaviours are temporally coordinated with the adult (Jaffe et al. 2001). This has the effect that the parent engages with the infant in communicative acts in which the infant is seen as a partner in conversation. Parental perception of the infant as a communicator results in variations of pitch of voice when addressing the preverbal baby. This can be illustrated with the use of 'real' and 'rhetorical' questions.

The function of question

When analysing the pitch of voice in real and rhetorical questions addressed to an infant aged 1–16 months, as shown in Chapter 8, Reissland (1998) found that around 15 months of age real and rhetorical yes–no questions were distinguished through pitch of voice. Hence, by 15 months of age, parents take into account what they believe the child to be capable of 'understanding' at some level not only by modifying their infant-directed speech generally (e.g. Ferrier 1978), but also, more specifically, by varying the pitch of voice depending on the type of question asked. At this age rhetorical questions were asked more playfully, indicated by the higher pitch. Given that a question will usually indicate a switch of roles (Schlegloff 1979), one function of the difference in pitch between real and rhetorical questions at 15 months might be to indicate turns or non-turns in conversations.

Regarding older children, Bergin and Bergin (1999) argued that adults influence the child's emotional interpretation by the control strategies they use in everyday discipline encounters that occur during routines. These routine interactions or frames provide the context for development of self-control, which leads not only to compliance by the child when being asked to do something, but also to internalization of societal values. Bergin (1987) found that reasoning with children during discipline is correlated with compliance and pro-social behaviours even in preverbal toddlers. Bergin (1987) argued that the most important component of the discipline encounter is how the child interprets his or her feelings.

How does language change over time during emotional exchanges between the father and his daughter? In order to answer this question, the father's conversations with his daughter, while she was on the changing table, were examined. Furthermore, the ability and willingness to comply with a request develops over time. The question of how this effective dialogic interaction is established at birth and followed up in the preverbal period is discussed in this chapter. Although speech varies as a function of infant age and communicative abilities (Stern et al. 1982; Broerse and Elias 1994; Kitamura and Burnham 2003), suggesting that the use of child-directed language is motivated by a desire to feel in communication with the infant (Brown 1977; Snow 1977), certain tasks such as getting dressed have to be accomplished from birth. The use of language in order to persuade a child to comply with demands has to reflect the child's language skills. However, in spite of her virtually non-existing language ability, the father uses rhetorical devices from birth in order to persuade his daughter to comply with his demands.

In order to determine the way in which the father uses rhetoric to induce the baby to cooperate with the task of getting dressed, the frequency of the use of pronouns was analysed over the first 15 months. Instances in which the father talked to his daughter about the task of getting dressed and used the pronouns 'I', 'you' or 'we' were counted as a percentage of utterances used while getting her dressed. Furthermore, the frequency of the first person plural, given its rhetorical use to mean either 'I', 'you' or 'we', was analysed. Lastly, taking as an example 'one frame' or 'interaction ritual' (e.g. Fogel et al. 2002) in which the father talked about socks, will be followed in terms of the infant's development from passive recipient to an interested conversational partner.

The use of 'I' and 'you'

The development of Toto's ability to distinguish the self 'I' from the other 'you' was tested by analysing her father's changing use of 'I' and 'you' in conversation with her from 1 to 15 months of age. There was a significant positive correlation between the mean frequency of using 'I' as a percentage of the text analysed and the age of the baby. As Toto grew older so there was more use of 'I', indicating that Toto's father referred more often to himself as his daughter matured. In contrast there was no significant correlation between Toto's age and use of 'you'. Hence, the father's use of 'you' did not change over time. Rather comparing the use of 'I' with the use of 'you', the 'you' is used by the father significantly more often at all ages of his daughter. The 'I' was used a mean percentage of 1.13 times per conversation while speaking to his daughter whereas 'you' was used with a mean percentage of 6.12 times per conversation, indicating that Toto's father addressed his daughter more often than he referred to himself while talking to her.

In terms of the use of 'we' as rhetorical device meaning 'I', 'you' or 'we', her father used the inclusive 'we' from the start of the recordings. In fact, the 'we' meant 'I', at the earlier ages.

When trying to dress his daughter in a shirt at 1 month, her father says:

> Now *we* have to put another hand in there. Oh, come on now. A little bit of cooperation would be great. It takes two to put on a shirt, you know.

At 5 weeks of age he told her:

> Yea, I know it's always a terrible war, mm. But I think that this time you might be a bit more cooperative, OK. Last time *we* got ourselves tied into knots, I admit. But this time maybe . . .; so I hope you're going to be in good spirits.

It is only at around the age of 6 months that the father started to use 'we' with the meaning of 'you'. For example, at 6 months the father said after dressing Toto:

> Mission accomplished. *We*'re all dressed now.

Another example is at 8 months where the father uses 'we' in terms of 'you' when he says:

That's it. I was interested to hear you practising your German this morning, Toto. Yes, you were saying nein, nein, nein. I heard you in bed this morning. Toto you don't have much to say this morning. Shall I turn the tape off until you're more loquacious? OK, let's get dressed first OK and then *we* can crawl around, huh. Yea, well perhaps not crawl; *we* can manoeuvre ourselves, can't *we*? That's what *we* do. You're a little manoeuvrer.

Six months is also the age at which the father started to use 'we' as a first person plural referring to him and his daughter or him and her mother, such as when talking about what is there for breakfast in the house:

Yeah, yeah, got to get ready for breakfast now. Want some breakfast? We have stodge, uh hum.

Another example at 6 months of age is:

OK, shall I turn it off Toto? Anything you've to add, to your memoirs before *we* go back to the kitchen? Anything you wish to add? I'll take some of the crumbs with us, m?

When talking about the need for dressing, the father says:

Yea, these are called clothes Toto and they keep us warm in winter; and it indicates that *we*'re civilized. Yea, unless *we*'re in St Tropez; perhaps *we* could holiday in St Tropez this summer. Would you like that?

The father used 'we' in three different senses. First, the use of 'we' meaning 'I' depending on age in months could be observed in 65 per cent of the tape recordings, starting from the first recording at 4 weeks of age with 108 times in which the father said 'we' but meant 'I'. The second most frequent use of 'we' meaning 'we' as the first person plural started at around 6 months of age and could be observed at all following ages in 38 per cent of the recordings. Third, the use of 'we' meaning 'you' was least frequently observed starting from 6 months of age in 30 per cent of the recordings. In sum, in the first few months the personal pronoun plural 'we' took on the meaning of 'I'. Only later at around 6 months did the father change the meaning of 'we' into either meaning 'you', or indicating the first person plural in terms of 'you and I' or 'Mummy and I'.

Putting on socks: what routines can tell us about development

The following analysis concerned changes in the father's use of personal pronouns occurring in a dyadic context in order to identify changes in the child's emotional maturity through the father's comments. Specifically, the father's speech referring to his daughter's actions were analysed in what Fogel et al. (2002) called a frame of interaction, namely while the father was engaged in dressing his daughter's feet with socks.

The father referred to Toto's socks from the first days of dressing her and hence made 'socks' an interesting topic of conversation. For example, when she was just 2 months old, he referred to her socks as shown in the following conversation:

> We've got the teddy bear (her jump suit with a bear motif) to put on and then your zero sized socks.

By 4 months of age, he told her to choose her socks by kicking the pair she liked best, such as:

> Choose your socks. Red, yellow, blue, green. Yellow, OK. Yellow socks, how pretty.

At 6 months of age the father recorded:

> Yea, so we have to choose our socks now, OK? So, if you have dark blue trousers and a bright red shirt; oh you have a lot of socks. You can have white socks. You can have yellow socks. You can have green socks, pink socks, dark blue socks and royal blue socks. What do you think? Green great! Fantastic choice; green with blue and bright red. Yes Toto, very original choice Toto.

At 8 months of age, this game turned around and Toto took control, as a recording testifies where the father complained:

> Perhaps I'll put different socks on, since I don't know how I'm gonna get those off you.

Later he said:

Who took this sock off? Who took this sock off? I've got something for you. You don't have to take yet another sock off, just play with your clown!

This was also the age (8 months) that the father reported Toto's use of 'nein' meaning no when he said: 'Yes, you were saying nein, nein, nein, nein.' This game of taking the socks off lasted for several weeks and the father showed his impatience at times. For example, at 10 months her father said:

Shall we put some socks on, yea? That's a sock. You don't have to pull it off immediately. I know you can pull them off if you want to but you don't have to Toto.

At 11 months the father remarked:

You've already taken your socks off. I put them on – you take them off, we'll be here for hours Toto.

When Toto is 1 year old the father was not amused any more by her actions and asked:

Shall we start this silly 'put the socks on' routine? And you can take it off?

Just a few days later he was surprised and exclaimed:

Boy Toto, you're actually trying to put socks on now. That's clever!

Hence, this account of dressing his daughter's feet with socks shows that the father introduced a topic of interest, which, in the present example, is her socks. In the first few months the father was well in control and happy to let his daughter influence the choice of socks to be worn by kicking her legs and apparently choosing their colour. Once she 'understood' that her father was interested in her socks, she herself showed that interest. At that time, namely at around 8 months of age, the 'we' of a common goal became a definite 'you' and 'I' as the father and daughter at that time had different goals, because she asserted her new-found interest by pulling her socks off. She was happy to play along with their conflicting aims until, at around 1 year of age, she surprised her father by trying to put the socks on rather than pulling them off.

Emotional intelligence in communicative frames

The first conversations adults have with infants from birth relate directly to the differentiation of the 'I' from the 'you', by distinguishing verbally the 'I' from the 'you'. This distinction is accompanied by the movement from being a passive recipient of the conversation at the earlier age to becoming an active partner in the communicative exchange. The present study followed this development of emotional intelligence in the context of communicative frames. Fogel et al. (2002) suggested that the dialogical self develops systematically over the first 18 months of life. In the present study the father's comments to his daughter while getting her dressed were followed from birth to 15 months of age, that is the age when the child can utter 'No' and hence arguably has differentiated the aims of the self from the aims of the other.

A clear progression could be discerned in the topic of interest introduced by the father, her socks. Once she 'understood' that her father was interested in socks she herself showed that interest. In the first few months, this 'frame' was used creatively, in that the interactions were constructed by creatively building a consensus. Hence, the father as well as his daughter appeared well in control and happy with their roles: the father offering a choice by dangling the socks in front of his daughter's feet and the daughter being free to choose by kicking her legs and apparently choosing their colour. However, this creative framing became rigid as time progressed, at around 8 months of age, when the 'we' of a common goal defined by the father as choosing socks and complied with by the daughter became a definite 'you' and 'I' having different goals. At this time, the daughter asserted a new-found interest, pulling off her socks, which was in conflict with her father's goal of putting them on her feet. The conflict continued until around 1 year of age, when the daughter changed the rigid frame by surprising her father with a new ability that is, trying to put on the socks rather than pulling them off.

In sum, there is a development from creative frame use to rigid frame use by the father. This change of creative to rigid frame use leads to the development of a creative frame use by the child and with that development to a resolution of the conflict. As the child started to perceive why the father was not amused by her opposition and that this opposition resulted in negative affect, she not only showed an increasing understanding of another's emotions but also found a way of gaining approval. She did this by indicating in her behaviour that she knew what was required of her, and she began to be able to act on this requirement as was expressed by the father's approval when he said: 'Boy Toto, you're actually trying to put socks on now. That's clever!'

Personal pronoun use has been analysed in terms of children's cognitive development. Michael Lewis and Ramsey (2004) examined personal pronoun use in relation to pretend play and self-recognition, in young children. They found that at the age of 15 months, children who used personal pronouns were able to recognize themselves in a mirror, compared to children who did not use personal pronouns. Self meta-representation, sometimes referred to as the mental state or the idea of 'me', involves the knowledge of the recursive relation 'I know that I know' as opposed to the non-recursive relation 'I know' that defines the sense of agency present at younger ages (Lewis 1995, 2001). In the present study, the father used the second person pronoun irrespective of the infant's age. In contrast, the use of the first person pronoun 'I' showed an age-related trend. As the baby grew older, so the father referred more often to himself as the 'I' as differentiated from the 'you'. This tendency was analysed in terms of the use of the first person plural, which serves as a rhetorical device to create closeness or distance between the speaker and the listener. Trevarthen and Hubley (1978) argued that a young infant's experience of 'primary intersubjectivity' is established in these proto-dialogues between adult and child and is reflected in the present study where from 1 to 6 months of age 'we' meant 'I', the father.

Trevarthen and Hubley (1978) suggested that in the second half of the first year, from around 6 months of age, 'secondary intersubjectivity' arises, in which the self emerges as part of a mutually regulated interaction. The onset of intentional communication, between 9 and 12 months of age, is marked by the emergence of so-called deictic gestures as well as by the use of word-like sounds for communicative purposes (e.g. Bates et al. 1975; Masur 1983). Deictic gestures such as pointing or showing are often used accompanied by word-like sounds (e.g. the baby points and vocalizes 'da' to direct attention to an interesting object), and subsequently by words. This secondary intersubjectivity was reflected in the present study by the use of 'we' meaning 'you' and hence distancing of the father when he spoke to his daughter, which occurred from around 6 months of age. The daughter's use of 'nein' or 'no' was recorded at that time of most conflict between father and daughter.

After 12 months of age, this form of intersubjectivity becomes increasingly symbolic. Between 12 and 15 months of age children start using a new type of gesture, called representational or symbolic (e.g. Acredolo and Goodwyn 1988). Different from deictic gestures, whose referent can be interpreted only by looking at the context, these new gestures represent a specific referent and thus their meaning does not change with context (e.g. child waves her hand meaning 'bye-bye'). Approximately at the same age range, children produce their first words in order to regulate social interaction, saying 'hello' and 'bye-bye' (Bloom 1973). This is also the time when in the present study the conflict concerning different aims in the wearing of socks seemed to subside, and instead of pulling off her socks Toto tried to put them on. In terms of emotional intelligence, according to Salovey and Grewal (2005) in their four-branch model of emotional intelligence, the skills needed to show emotional intelligence cannot exist outside of the social context in which they operate. Most importantly, in order to use these skills, a person must be aware of what is considered appropriate behaviour by the people with whom he or she interacts.

In summary, in this chapter the development of emotionally intelligent behaviour by Toto could be observed in two aspects of interaction, the changing use of personal pronouns in the father's speech as he perceives her developing abilities and the child's changing behaviour recounted by her father, in view of the father's emotional reactions.

10 Teasing and emotional development:

Father: So what do you have to say for yourself?
Toto: Haa.
Father: You don't have much to say. A woman of few words, m?
You speak softly and carry a big stick.

How does teasing relate to emotional development and the development of emotional intelligence?

One of the special features of fathers in contrast to most mothers is their propensity to engage in verbal and nonverbal teasing with their children (Hopper et al. 1983; Pecheux and Labrell 1994; Reissland 1998). Teasing can elicit a positive bond or communion with the person and hence reflects an intimate bond in a relationship (Eder 1991; Sharkey 1992), or it may be hostile (Warm 1997). Teasing behaviour is usually described in negative terms in the popular media, and is often considered to be synonymous with or a precursor to bullying. In fact, both positive and negative forms of teasing exist. It has been defined in a number of ways, for example, as 'a diverse set of verbal and non-verbal actions that share in common a combining of the elements of aggression, humour, and ambiguity' (Shapiro et al. 1991: 460). Eisenberg (1986) described teasing more simply as mock insults. Teasing generally involves features of novelty, unpredictability and cognitive destabilization. That is, teasing is a stimulus that contradicts previously fixed rules or expectations (Pecheux and Labrell 1994). Labrell (1994) suggests that this provocative play between parent and child may involve a positive overture, for example a parent offering a desired object to a child. However, by offering the toy and then by frustrating the child by not handing it over, negative reaction can be created in the child and then teasing may become a negative experience, which can result in a child's loss of self-esteem and feelings of rejection (Leary et al. 1998). What effect playful teasing has on the infant depends on how sensitive the parent is to the emotional reactions of the baby. In infancy, for example, teasing the baby in a peek-a-boo game or teasing the child with dangling a toy just out of reach has to be finely timed in order to elicit laughter rather than tears of frustration from the target of the tease. Specifically, measures of parental sensitivity, such as interactional synchrony (Isabella et al. 1989), harmony (Schölmerich et al. 1995) and emotional responsiveness (Tronick 1989) all indicate that sensitive mothering has an effect on the infant's emotional reactions.

In infancy, teasing through provocative play between parent and child may be positive. However, if the tension created in play elicits fear or anger in the child, teasing may become a negative experience. This early negative interaction, if continued, may be perceived by the child to devalue him or her and thus imply interpersonal rejection (Leary et al. 1998). Understanding 'teasing' behaviour is a developmental process, in that children have to learn that certain behaviours are not to be taken seriously. This implies that children have to learn about language and behaviour which cannot be taken at face value or literally. A weakness in the ability to understand non-literal language, such as humour, irony and teasing, is one of the aspects that distinguishes individuals on the autistic spectrum from normally developed individuals (Kasari and Rotheram-Fuller 2005). Hence, teasing behaviour allows an analysis of how the baby is taught about emotional self-awareness and ultimately the development of emotional intelligence in the baby.

This chapter traces the development of teasing from the time that Toto gets teased to the time that she teases her father and shows that teasing can be a pleasant experience; it is the basis for the child to become able to interact in her environment in an emotionally mature way. Teasing might be a way to further emotional intelligence in the baby. Specifically, teasing helps the baby to increase aspects of emotional intelligence, namely emotional self-awareness, as described by Salovey and Mayer (1990). Emotional self-awareness is an ability which includes recognizing, naming and understanding the cause of emotions experienced. A child who is able not only to identify feeling 'bad' but also to say that he or she is angry, hurt, jealous, sad or scared in various contexts shows emotional intelligence by being able to differentiate finely between different emotions. The same is true for positive emotions. The analysis of teasing behaviours and reactions to teasing permits an analysis of the developmental progress of emotional intelligence. In infancy, some forms of play, such as peek-a-boo, create tension between participants by incorporating some form of ambiguity. This tension created by the ambiguity of the interaction may elicit a positive response, such as laughter, from the baby. The infant can, however, also perceive teasing negatively, which creates an aversive reaction in the child. Creating tension in play relates to the concept of teasing, defined as an act that is directed to achieve affective consequences for the target of the action (Keltner et al. 2001).

There are indications of gender differences in the use of, response to and acceptability of teasing behaviours. For example, in a study of teasing between romantic partners, men and women teased one another in similar ways, but women found that being the target of teasing was much more aversive (Keltner et al. 1998). When asked, mothers deplore their husbands' teasing interactions with their children (Pecheux and Labrell 1994)

There are gender differences not only in teasing behaviour by mothers or fathers but also in boys and girls. Boys, in contrast to girls, demonstrate more teasing behaviour and greater use of language for purposes of humour (Mooney et al. 1991; Lampert 1996), which is a pattern similar to that of adult males. These same gender differences are also reflected in mothers and fathers teasing their babies. A number of researchers found that one of the special features of fathers' behaviour with their children is the tendency for fathers to engage in verbal and nonverbal teasing with their children (Hopper et al. 1983; Pecheux and Labrell 1994). Based on a review of papers on child-directed speech, there seems to be very little research on maternal teasing. One study by Miller (1986) found some teasing by mothers of working-class background. Reports of verbal teasing by fathers have generally been limited to instances of jocular name-calling, such as 'knuckle-head'. These instances of rather negative teasing have been directed towards sons rather than daughters. However, teasing in the present study of father–daughter interactions is much more varied and one can find teasing involving innuendo, her language and physical limitations as well as appeasement through teasing.

While teasing may appear to be non-social and counterproductive behaviour, fathers' teasing may serve positive purposes for the child (Reddy 1991). In terms of cognitive development, teasing with its unpredictability can stimulate playfulness and vigilance. The destabilizing function of teasing may provoke cognitive growth in much the same way that fathers' lack of verbal fine-tuning can serve as a catalyst to advances in communicative competence. Teasing can be linked to the child's development of theory of mind. According to Stern (1985), successful recognition of teasing behaviour requires the ability to correctly guess what is in the mind of the other person. Teasing may have a role in the development of other language skills as well. For example, Ortony et al. (1985) reported that inner-city children who engaged in playful insult-exchange games ('sounding' or 'playing the dozens') were better able to comprehend metaphoric language. Teasing experience can also serve social purposes, as a vehicle by which males establish affiliation with one another. All-boy groups demonstrate various forms of playful teasing such as heckling, joking or making mock threats (Maltz and Borker 1982). Done in a friendly way, teasing can establish and reinforce group cohesion (Kyratzis and Guo 1996). As a type of humour or verbal wit, teasing is a device for establishing and reordering social hierarchies (Keltner et al. 1998). Thus, 'a child who cannot share jokes with other children or does not know how to tease or be teased, lacks important aspects of communicative competence' (Ely and Gleason 1995: 267). In these many ways, fathers' teasing can prepare children for the give and take of teasing that underlies social affiliation, friendship rituals and communicative patterns encountered with males outside the family. In this chapter I examine teasing behaviour in the context of emotional development by establishing the range of teasing behaviours in various contexts and the change of these teasing behaviours over time.

Teasing involving innuendo

One type of verbal teasing involves innuendo. This type of teasing could be observed from the first few days after birth such as in the following example.

The father needs to clean his daughter at 1 month of age:

Father: Good Lord! Good Lord! Say no more, OK. I don't think with all that this little tub of water will work. We'll have to bring out the garden hose.
Toto: Ah ah.

Later in the year the father returns to teasing her about changes of clothes:

Father: Yeah, I should've gotten that washing machine, yeah, definitely. I should've gotten that washing machine.
Toto   (babbling): Airrrrrurr airrr eh airrr.

Father: Because one mistake, one flaw in my plan is that you are too young to do your own washing when you want it.

Talking about the need for toilet training at 3 months old, the father states:

Father: So life goes on. All intellectual effort is stopped in this house until we get you toilet trained and my desk can become a desk again and not a changing table. Until then I don't see how I'm going to write another word.

Another time the father remarks:

Father: Did you sleep well in your bed last night? It's a nice little bed, there, isn't it? Even though it looks a bit like a prison from the inside, mm? All those bars. Yea, those bars.

The father continues the theme of prison with the following tease:

Father: OK. Next stage, clothes. It's a cool and a cloudy day. So what do you want? Oh I see, you like the look of these stripes. Oh, those stripes drive you crazy? Or do you want your duckies? Prison stripes it is. Yea, with your red prison stripes, you'll look so neat. And then when you go take your nap this afternoon, in your crib, in your new crib, behind all those bars, why people will think, it's Sing Sing, Alcatraz, Wormwood Scrubs, yea just like a like a little prisoner.

Teasing involving sleep

At 10½ months, Toto is still being teased about her sleep:

Father: Did you have a difficult night, he? Did we keep you awake?
Toto: Ejda.
Father: Were we the ones who woke you up at 12:30, 1:30, 3:30 and 6:30? Admittedly, it wasn't a record last night. It was only four times. It wasn't a world record, it wasn't a personal best, just the normal.
Toto: Eijajej.
Father: That was the evening of the 13th, dare I say the early morning of the 14th, a Tuesday 1989.

Or in the following example where her father refers to her problematic sleeping patterns:

Father: After a pub crawl Toto returns to base. It takes two people to change Toto, sometimes it takes three and we have to call in reinforcements. Shall we call in the Grasers from next door or some Olympic wrestlers perhaps?
Toto: Eheh.
Father: Shall we call in some Olympic wrestlers?
Toto: Eheh.
Toto   (cries).
Father: A typical night, a typical night.
Toto   (cries).
Father: I don't know if I want you as an assistant professor in my department.
Toto   (cries).
Father: Give her some Calpol, sleepy time tea, a wiff of opium.
Toto: Eheh.
Father: And if that doesn't work a sledge hammer.

When she has reached 16 months, sleeping is still a concern which her father raises by teasing her while reading a book on the topic of sleeping.

Father: Night time.
Toto: Urur urur.
Father: Night time. A moving tale of a child that goes to bed without any difficulty for its parents. Brings tears to the eyes doesn't it?
Toto: Duna. Adu.
Father: Wanna read it? Look. This is the town. And in the town there is a street. And in the street there's a house. Look there's a boy upstairs playing with a dog and a ball and a kitty cat. In the house there's a room (whispers) hoo hoo hoo in the room can you see a tiny baby fast asleep.
Toto: Dur.
Father: Yeah she's asleep. Mustn't disturb her.
Toto: Ur ur a dur.
Father: Another read? This is really a gripping tale. A tale. A baby fast asleep. I didn't know they came that way. Night time. This is called the step by step night time book. Hahaha (laughs). Completely ineffectual, hey Toto?

Teasing involving language or physical limitations

When Toto is about 3 months old her father teases her about her limited language:

Father: What are your thoughts?
Toto (babbling): Eh. Eh eh hairr reh eh.
Father: Oh I see, difficult to express what's on your mind, is it? You don't quite have the words, is that it?

Another example of this type of teasing comes when he teases her about having hiccups:

Father: Yeah, sort of interrupts the syntax, doesn't it?
Toto (hiccup): Err . . .
Father: Yeah, you've hardly got the subject out . . .
Toto (hiccup).
Father: One or two propositional phrases . . .
Toto (hiccup).
Father: . . . and then comes a hiccup! And then you gotta stop and reconsider before you get onto the verb . . .
Toto (hiccup): Aah hee.
Father: . . . and by the time you've got the auxiliary and main verb out and about to say the indirect object then a hiccup comes. What you ought to do perhaps is to arrange your hiccups so they serve as punctuation marks to what you say.
Toto: Aargh.
Father: Did you know Toto that 30 per cent of utterances are in the imperative mode and not the declarative mode. Yea declarative comes much later. They forgot to look at babies' utterances; they say things mostly in the imperative, I think.
Toto: Aggaa.
Father: You do a lot of talking in the imperative Toto.

It is not only being able to talk but also how Toto interacts with books which is a topic used to tease Toto such as when her father says:

Father: We can have a read perhaps. How about 'The duck says quack' or maybe 'One to ten count again', that's a nice book, OK? And then perhaps a book to chew. What would you like to chew on? 'Teatime' or 'On the barn'? Let's chew on 'Teatime' that seems an appropriate title. Yea, the medium is the message; the message is the medium.

When she is 16 months old, her father teases her about her language. Toto babbles while getting dressed: 'Dada'.

Father: That's it, now don't you look smart? You got little bear here. There's little bear. Your bear shirt. So now when you go growl, growl.
Toto: Urowyurr.
Father: You go grow, growl, everyone is gonna understand you.
Toto: Dur.

Around that time her father also addresses her bilingual abilities:

Father: Ball yes. And what's it in German Toto?
Toto: Dar.
Father: Ball, yeah. Toto you know two languages, so perfectly.
Toto: Bah.
Father: Are you so pleased for yourself? Perfectly bilingual as far as the word ball is concerned.

Her father also teases her about her first steps to walking:

Father: Yea, you're 10 and a half months old, m? Ten and a half months old and yesterday evening you stood for the first time.
Toto: Ahwau.
Father: Yapp, you stood for about point two seconds.
Toto: He.
Father: Well it's a personal best! It's a start isn't it? Maybe in a few days you will be able to stand for point four seconds.
Toto: Dede.

Teasing involving appeasement

Toto cries. Father, squeezing a soft toy making a squeaking noise, says:

Father: Why it's the Volkswagen beeping its horn. It wants to overtake something. Chump into the mouth. You know

Toto, I read somewhere in the Guinness Book of Records, there's a gentleman in Wales who over 20 years ate an entire lorry. And you want to eat in one evening an entire Volkswagen. I hope you don't get indigestion, later tonight.

When Toto is 6 months old, her father reports:

Father: You helped me so much. You cleaned up the corridor and then you helped me with the dishes and then you helped me put all the clothes away. Toto, what spirit of self-sacrifice. And you didn't complain once.
Toto (whining).
Father: Well, perhaps once, but not twice. Well maybe twice. But not, well maybe three times. Not to mention the time in the kitchen you flashed the yellow card, warning me that once more and I'd get the red card and would be sent off the pitch.

When Toto has reached 16 months of age, her father teases her in order to make light of a fall:

Father: What's that, what's that? Oh you bit your lip Toto. Oh did you hurt yourself there? Did you fall and hurt yourself?
Toto: Daiuu.
Father: Is that why you were kicking the floor the other day?
Toto: Dadaia.
Father: That aggressive floor, leaps up off the ground and sort of hits you around like that.

Other instances of teasing reported in the literature relate to play styles. For example, Pecheux and Labrell (1994) studied the play styles of mothers and fathers with their 16-month-old infants. Fathers teased their children by placing objects in the way of their children's goals or by physically redirecting them away from a desired goal or object.

Verbal teasing involving nicknames

When she has reached 22 months of age:

Father: You are a nuisance, huh?
Toto: Nuisance.

Father: A nuisance.

Toto: A nuisance.

Father: A complete and utter nuisance. Yeah. Otherwise known for short as Troublemaker. That's why we use so much brute force. Hum?

When Toto goes through a very clingy stage and insists on being near Mummy or Daddy all the time her Daddy calls her his 'little shadow' such as in the following example:

Father: I'll just get my reading spectacles, OK? Daddy comes right back.

Toto   (not happy): Dah.

Father: Yeah.

Toto   (insisting on going with him): With!

Father   (accepting): Come little shadow.

Toto expresses that she is not called little shadow but 'Toto' and that she wants to be read to: 'Reading. More.' Her father complies: 'Yeah'.

Toto: Read!

Father: So little shadow, what do you want to read?

Toto   (insisting): Read.

Father: Yeah, well bring your book for Daddy. Bring a book, and we'll read.

Toto 'teasing' Daddy

As Toto grows older she attempts to tease, such as in the following example in which the teasing starts with her Daddy saying:

> Those are Mummy's papers I think Toto. Hm? Are you reading Mummy's papers? Are you reading all about child development? Hmm? So you can develop yourself faster and faster? Is it possible? Hey Totissimo.

Toto responds by teasing him and trying to write on Mummy's papers and Daddy attempts to prevent her from doing it asking:

Father: What are you doing? Oh don't do that Toto. No no no no. Get your paper; get the paper from the drawer, OK?

Toto	(asking): Da da?
Father:	Yeah get that paper, OK? You can write on that paper.
Toto	(asking for clarification): This?
Father:	That there, yeah. Oh! Yes, your crayons. But get your paper as well. Get your paper.
Toto:	Yes. Da. Dada? Paper?
Father:	Oh yes! That's a nice little book, you can draw on that!
Toto:	Toto!
Father:	What did she do?
Toto:	Naughty!
Father:	Were you naughty? What did you do?
Toto:	Do.
Father:	Oh I see, you did that did you? You were a bit naughty the other day weren't you? Hmm?
Toto	(responding proudly): Da.
Father:	You were a bit naughty.

Later while playing at constructing a house with Lego:

Toto:	Da!
Father:	I know. Are you being good or are you being naughty?
Toto:	Naughty.
Father:	You're being naughty. Exactly.

In another example her father says when drawing a house:

Father:	Hey little Toto! Mhm. I've almost got this establishment now finished.
Toto	(interrupting): Da! Da!.
Father:	How? – Toto! You are being naughty now, hm? That's not good.
Toto	(trying to make amends): Peter Rabbit. Peter Rabbit, urn?
Father:	Yeah. You can do one of Peter Rabbit, come on. You can draw with a little crayon, look?

Toto gets more adventurous as time passes, such as in the following example when her mother is preparing Toto's bubble bath, her father asks: 'What's Mummy doing? Toto says: 'Ah'. Father explains: 'She's doing the bath, yes. Toto exclaims: 'Toto!' Father specifies: 'Toto's bath.' Toto says: 'Yes.' Father: 'With bubble bath, huh?' Toto remembers her naughty behaviour in the afternoon: 'Bubble bath. Drink, drink.' Father: 'Hm? Drink? Yes you drank some bubbles didn't you? You drank the soap. Hmm? The washing up soap didn't you? This afternoon? Tasty stuff wasn't it?'

No sooner have they talked about the last naughty incident, Toto thinks of the next thing she can do:

Toto:	Book!
Father:	What book?
Toto:	Da!
Father:	No. You know, that's a no-no don't you?
Toto:	(teasing): Da?
Father:	You know that's a no-no. You're not dumb.
Toto	(asking innocently): Dumb?
Father:	You are not dumb.
Toto:	Dumb?
Father:	No. You know you're not dumb.
Toto:	No?
Father:	A bit obstreperous. Hm? Yes, do you want to show your Mummy what you did? Where was Toto naughty?
Toto	(proudly): Is da! Da!

When Toto is a bit older and is drawing with her Daddy, he says: 'Be careful now, huh? You be careful, you have to do it only on paper.' Toto agrees: 'Yes.' Father: 'Only on paper. That's a pretty colour, isn't it?' Toto asks: 'Toto'? Father says: 'Yea, there's Toto.' Toto then teases her father pointing saying: 'Da' and her father says: 'Yea there's Toto.' Again she points, asking 'Da?' Father asks: 'Yea?' And Toto makes explicit what she means by saying: 'Finger!' Father replies: 'No paper, not finger!'

In sum first efforts of 'teasing' relate to overstepping boundaries by doing forbidden things and hence result in an unending effort of chaos control by parents. These are often called the terrible twos in which the child does not yet distinguish what is a tease and could result in laughter and what is naughty behaviour eliciting anger in her parents. Teasing becomes more explicit as language develops and she can clarify to her father what she means.

Teasing as we have seen occurs mostly in situations of conflict (Keltner et al. 2001). Although the very earliest teasing situations concern conflict which is situational (e.g. father trying to cope with difficult situations while changing her nappy) rather than interpersonal. Teasing is evident from the first few weeks of life and involves many different areas, including Toto's emerging abilities from her early steps to communication to her later efforts of walking. Even the very first teasing events include innuendo. Hence her father uses complex social conventions at a time when his daughter is too young to understand them, reflecting the general observation that paternal interactions with their children are complex and unexpected. Evidence suggests that fathers' nonverbal play behaviour may benefit their children in various ways. Compared to mothers, fathers' play behaviour is more complex as well as being more physical and boisterous (Lamb et al. 1982; Fagot 1997). It is also more unpredictable and novel (Pecheux and Labrell 1994). Even fathers' singing style with their children evidences unpredictability. Trehub et al. (1997) found that while mothers tended to sing stereotypic, child-oriented, simple songs ('Twinkle twinkle' or 'Itsy bitsy spider'), fathers altered popular or folk songs, creating complex songs for their children. Fathers' play behaviour is less likely to involve the thematic play (playing store, playing school) that is more typical of mothers. In many ways these behaviours echo fathers' verbal style with their children in its less scripted, less predictable character. Fathers' play style has been linked to infants' increased exploratory behaviour, both in unfamiliar environments (Feldman et al. 1997) and with unfamiliar adults (Kromelow et al. 1990).

   The developmental progress of teasing has not been studied in very young babies. The present observation indicates that teasing behaviour is one-sided at the earliest teasing stages but becomes over time bidirectional in that Toto not only seems to laugh at her father's teasing but also starts to tease herself. There is a fine line, which Toto has to negotiate, between teasing her father and being naughty. This process, however, leads to her learning about and evaluating emotional reactions of others and hence contributes to her developing emotional intelligence.

11 From 'social smile' to laughter
How positive emotions develop

Father to Toto (2½ months old): 'OK, I'm gonna smile and then you're gonna smile. Ready?'

How to explain a smile

Research on emotional development in infancy in general and laughter in particular provides a rich source of information concerning not only emotional but also cognitive development in infancy (Sroufe and Wunsch 1972). This idea relates to the argument that emotional intelligence plays an important role in determining a person's ability to succeed in life and directly influences a person's psychological well-being in terms of their emotional health. Explaining emotional experience might foster children's understanding of the breadth of a specific emotion, such as happiness, which is usually indicated by positive facial expressions, such as a smile. Some researchers (e.g. Sroufe 1995) argue that positive emotions in the first three months of life are related to the child experiencing the recognition of a visual stimulus (e.g. the father's face) with a relaxation in cognitive tension. As infants mature cognitively, they also grow emotionally and around 9 months of age, infants express more intense positive emotional feeling states, through smiling and laughter (e.g. Sroufe 1995). Hence, researchers such as Izard and Ackerman (2000) and Lewis (2000) see infant smiles as an index of joy. One function of the expression of joy is to maintain a close social tie with the person at whom the joyous expression is directed (e.g. Campos et al. 1994).

Research on smiling has been conducted mostly in the context of behavioural measurements. Smiles directed at another person, or 'social smiles' situated within parent–child interactions, can be used to measure behaviourally the degree of positive emotional engagement between baby and parent. Even though it is clear that facial expression of emotions occurs very early in life and that facial movements, such as widening of the mouth representing a smile, start already in fetal life, it is not clear what these behaviours signify. In terms of the dynamic systems approach to the function of social smiles, smiles are created interactively and vary over time (e.g. Camras 2000; Messinger et al. 1997). In this view, the child simultaneously experiences the physical and emotional effects of a smile and gives out signals to the social partner (Messinger and Fogel 2007).

The problem with labelling emotions

Elfenbein and Ambady (2002) argue that in spite of differences in culture, age or social background, many researchers seem to agree on the emotions signalled. In contrast, Russell et al. (2003) state that there is wide variation between research which suggests that emotional signals, such as a smile indicating happiness or a frown indicating anger, are agreed upon and research which does not find much correlation between the signal and the emotion felt. Haidt and Keltner (1999) found that the range of agreements depended on the specific emotion studied. Some emotions such as happiness seem to be more easily labelled than other emotions such as fear.

Adults interacting with babies have no problems in labelling facial expressions. Although they are able to produce emotion labels for babies' facial expressions, adult raters do not always agree on the identity of the emotion they label. Specifically, positive emotions seem to be easier to agree on compared with negative emotions. Yik et al. (1998) found that labelling pictures of babies as 'happy' they were able to record up to 98 per cent of correct labels from Canadian, Chinese and Japanese judges. Other emotion labels in contrast were less well identified. Given that emotion labels were produced for babies in specific situations such as playing with a baby, I argue here with others that emotional meaning grows in social interaction. In this chapter I examine one aspect of positive social emotions, namely the smile as labelled by the father during his interactions with his baby daughter, and demonstrate how positive emotional expressions change over time in terms of what elicits a smile and what makes the infant and her father laugh.

The function of smiles

Experience

Smiles have various functions. The process of smiling itself can contribute to the feeling state of experiencing joy (Soussignan 2002). In other words, the more you smile, the happier you feel. Another function of the smile is to act as a social signal. A smile attracts the attention of those around. From the first days of life, parents try to identify their infant's facial expression and label their emotions. In particular, positive emotional expressions, specifically smiles are attractive to parents as the following example shows.

When Toto is 4 weeks old, her father whispers: 'A smile, are you going to give me a smile? A social smile? Smile!' When he does not get any reactions, he says disappointedly: 'Oh, no smiles.'

In this context her father interprets his daughter's smile as expressing the emotion it is normally supposed to signal, namely happiness or joy. Although in the literature, we find a debate about what meanings we are supposed to attribute to facial expression of emotions, with some arguing that facial expressions show discrete emotions (e.g. Izard et al. 1983) and others saying that expressions of emotions do not represent true feeling states (e.g. Fernandez-Dols and Ruiz-Belda 1995), parents label emotions expressed by their infants. They do not question that a smile is really an index of happiness at 3 months of age, as the following example illustrates:

Father asks: 'Is Karina happy?' He replies for her saying, 'I am happy, yes'.

Another example is given when the father says: 'Are you pleased with yourself? What a smile!'

At this very early stage of development, infant smiles become linked to environmental stimulation, especially looking at a face when parents interact with their babies, which sets the stage for the 'social smile'. Researchers have observed how the developmental patterns unfold in the first few weeks of life. First, one can discern sequential patterns, in which an infant attends to a face, such as her father's face, followed by a big effort in concentrating on that face and finally smiling at the face. This sequence, according to Lavelli and Fogel (2005), indicates a social smile because it is often preceded by a period in which infants knit their brows. The brows then relax, which is interpreted as the behavioural expression of recognizing the face in view and finally a smile forms. In terms of behavioural markers, usually studied in the context of mother–infant engagement, mothers show fewer neutral facial expressions compared to their infants. Over time as infants develop, mothers increase not only the frequency with which they simultaneously smile but also the frequency with which they talk to their infants.

The child's well-being

Smiles do not only signal an emotion. They are also important indicators for a child's well-being. If a 'social' smile is missing, parents question why this should be the case as in the following example of the father talking to his daughter when she is around 6 months old:

'Mrs B says you haven't smiled. Mm? You haven't smiled for Memsahib yet today. She says you're very serious.'

The explanation for that serious behaviour might lie in the stars: 'Yeah. Maybe it's in the stars. We haven't seen your horoscope for a long time now. Yes. My little Taurus. Our little Taurus.'

Hence, adults recognize infant smiles from the earliest stage of life and parents question and interpret the lack of smiles. Furthermore, infant smiles expressed in certain contexts not only relate to environmental stimulation, but also indicate the infant's increasing cognitive development. For example, in the context of language learning the child's 'understanding' of labels given during daily routines is indicated by a smile, as the next extract illustration shows. The father interprets a smile in terms of his daughter's understanding of labelling routine occurrences such as the first meal of the day.

Father	(to mother): When I said 'Breakfast', she smiled (laughs) and she immediately took her fist out of her mouth in anticipation.
Father	(to Toto): Yes, 'breakfast', 'breakfast'. Is that the first word you're going to speak?
Toto:	Heh.
Father:	I think your first three words will be 'Breakfast', 'Lunch' and 'Dinner'.

Degrees of happiness

A further aspect of smiling concerns the intensity of the emotion expressed. The quality of emotions is labelled and varies from being labelled as 'placid' or content, 'a social smile', 'delight' and at its most extreme form 'laughter'.

When Toto is content her father said:

Hey! You're looking extremely passive and placid. Yea, aha, a little smile; a little smile, but not a big one. And no conversation! Sunday is your day of silence.

When she is around 4 months old, her father remarks on her social communication via a smile:

All these social smiles you're giving me are a nonverbal form of communication. But our present technology [meaning that only audiotapes were made] only allows for verbal communication.

In the following example, her father comments on her 'delight':

Father: We have things to do today.
Toto: Eh ah!
Father: Yea, you're delighted.
Toto: Eh!
Father: Their profits are up this quarter. You're making so much business for the Laundromat. Perhaps you get a commission.

The most positive expression of happiness is laughter and the father comments:

You have your laughter and your tears. Don't you? And your hiccups! Tears, laughter and hiccups.

The expression of this extreme form of happiness requires from Toto a specific vocalization rather than general noise, such as when he asks her to laugh and she makes a vocalization which does not meet his expectations:

Father: This is a wasted tape actually, isn't it? You haven't said beans. Are you going to say something? Have another laugh! Record another laugh for posterity.
Toto: Ehehe.
Father: That was a squeaking door routine.

Laughter, the most intense expression of positive emotions, occurs later on in development (e.g. Ambrose 1963; Ruch and Ekman 2001). Sroufe and Wunsch (1972), when analysing laughter in babies aged 4–6 months, 7–9 months and 10–12 months, found that the frequency of laughter increased with age. However, the items eliciting laughter also changed with age. Babies aged 7–9 months laughed mostly in response to auditory and tactile stimulation whereas 10–12-month-old babies laughed more in response to visceral and social stimulation such as playing tug or peek-a-boo, or chasing games such as in the following example

Toto is 13 months old and her father chases her in order to change her clothes:

Father: Oh, Toto come on. Hey. Where are you running off to?

Toto laughs. Father laughs.

This kind of chasing game results in extreme laughter or tears, such as in the following example:

Father: Hey, back onto the changing table. Back onto the changing table, please. Where are you off to?
Toto: Gag!
Father: Reinforcements, reinforcements!
Toto   (laughing).
Father: Reinforcements.
Toto   (crying).
Father: Now I've got you; reinforcements; OK, OK, you win, I lose, I lose. Watch it, don't run! You bumped into something. It's all right; I'm not chasing you any more. Escape OK, at a reasonable speed.
Toto: Eheh.

The changing context of a smile

The context of smiling changes as the child grows older. During the early period of emotional development, mood swings are very evident, as is shown in this example.

Toto is around 2½ months old:

Father: Six forty three p.m. and we're trying to establish why you can be so miserable one moment and so happy the next.

The type of actions which elicit labelling of positive emotions by the father changes with the age of the baby. In the first three months of his daughter's life, her father is amused by her hiccups, for example, and displays positive emotions which are mirrored by his daughter:

Yea, a bit difficult to talk with hiccups though. Yea, sort of interrupts the syntax, m? Yea, you've hardly got the subject out mm? One or two propositional phrases . . . and then comes a hiccup.

However, after the first few months of life, laughter is elicited though active engagement.

Laughter occurs in games such as peek-a-boo, as the recording when she is 5 months old documents:

Father: Peekaboo, peekaboo. Hello, hello, yea. I lost sight of you for a moment.
Toto   (happily babbling): Huhehehee.
Father: Boo.

Around the age of 6 months, it is clear that the baby now expresses positive emotions independent of her environment. She can be happy even if the world around her is falling apart, as in the following extract when the father says:

And while Memsahib is slowly going crazy and Babusahib is slowly getting more and more worried about his lectures. Only baby-doctor is quite happy; happily chewing the Volkswagen.

The independence of her own emotional state from others becomes more firmly established over time as the following example shows:

Toto   (squeaking and laughing).
Father: Some babies, you know, are tired at this hour; they know it's time to go to bed. But for others the party just begins, he? Yea, isn't that true Toto?

In terms of learning how to cope with emotional upsets, that is to establish mature emotional functioning in everyday encounters, the father teaches methods or coping strategies. He teaches Toto that laughing about a 'sad' situation helps one to cope with it.

Toto is around 13 months old and has fallen over, which makes her upset:

Father: Toto, if you climb up on the toy chest I can't do anything else, but catch you when you fall. Ooops, another time.

Toto	(crying).
Father:	Oh come on, oh did that hurt? Did that catch you on the bean? Shall we kick the floor now? Bum, bum bum.
Toto:	(laughing).

The father also teaches her about other people's perceptions of her actions. Some things are amusing and others are not funny, rather they are classed as naughty behaviours, which are not condoned. For example, Toto does some 'work' on her father's desk:

Father:	So, you've got the key for the letterbox. The only key for the letterbox, I might add.
Toto:	Uh dah. Uh huh.
Father:	You have the only key for the letterbox now.
Toto:	Uhuhah.

Mother in the background suggests that they should be copied.

Father:	I think if, if we didn't have a daughter, it wouldn't be necessary. I think we ought to actually.
Toto:	Ahahah.
Father:	Yeah, an ounce of prevention is a pound of cure.

Toto then reaches for the next important paper and father says jokingly: 'Those, oh yeah, let's throw away my receipts for this dry cleaning.'

Toto:	Dah.
Father:	Hum?
Toto:	Dah.
Father:	Why do you have to snoop around here Toto? Why do you have to snoop?
Toto:	De de deva va va vak.
Father:	Work?
Father	(to Mother): Oh, she really enjoys working.
Father	(laughing): Can't keep her away from it.
Toto:	Uh uh. Dah.
Father:	How can I get rid of you?
Toto:	Dah.
Father:	That is a lot of money.
Toto:	In havin.

Father: You don't have to have that. A little coin is good enough for you. Huh? (laughs) What are you? What trouble are you gonna get into now?

Toto: Dah.

Father: What's that?

Toto: Dah.

Father: Yeah, those are the receipts for my dry cleaning. If I lose them, I lose my trousers. OK? Let's put them right back, they're very important. Very important, they have to stay there.

After having been told that she cannot have one thing, Toto find the next, saying: 'Dah.' Her father explains: 'Those are envelopes.'

Toto: De Mummy?

Father: Well Mummy uses them, Daddy uses them, Toto uses them.

Toto: Huh.

Father: Hum? Those are airmail envelopes. If you want to send a letter to somebody on the North Pole, you use that envelope.

By around 1 year of age parents seem not to laugh any more about involuntary actions such as hiccups but they laugh about voluntary actions of their children. Parents are amused by voluntary actions, albeit unintentional mistakes children produce, such as in the example of falling over while learning to walk.

Father: Oh, you're a travelling man, are you? That's very good. Eight steps, nine, ten, eleven, twelve, thirteen, fourteen, plop. Fourteen steps and then plop!

Toto   (laughing).

Father: Fourteen steps and then you collapse.

Toto: Eehe.

Father: Yea that's what happens.

Another example eliciting laughter from the father concerns his daughter's verbal responses such as when he remarks: 'Yeah, I know, you're gonna screw up the whole operation, huh? I know you.' Toto replies: 'No', and her father laughs.

He also laughs about his daughter's use of words when she is 1 year and 9 months old and he asks her whether she is a gangster:

Father: That is your blouse.
Toto: Naee naee naee naee de park.
Father: You are turning into a gangster.
Toto: Gangster.
Father: Can you say I am a gangster?
Toto: Yeah.
Father   (laughing): You can?

In sum, in the first year of life, positive emotional expression is a developmental process, which progresses from smile to laughter. Especially at the younger age the infant does not laugh but seems to smile and her father labels these smiles. Later she is able to express laughter. According to Tracy and Robins (2008), emotion recognition is automatic and requires only minimal cognitive resources. However, even if adults can recognize emotions subliminally (Winkielman et al. 2005), there needs to be some developmental process, which allows the social construction of these emotions in specific contexts. In this chapter, I have demonstrated that emotional expression of the child changes over time and that the father labels these expressions for her and links them to what he perceives as appropriate social situations. Hence, by labelling the situations which make her laugh, she learns about events that make her happy, even though events which make the father and his daughter happy differ. This is indicated by the fact that in the context of father–daughter interactions, father and daughter laugh about different aspect of the situation. In spite of the fact that father and daughter laugh at different aspects of the situation, they are joined in laughter in the same context, which makes the laughter a social event.

12 Toto's experience of her father's death

Toto at 4 years old explains paradise to her dying father:

> It is very nice there. And we can fly up in the plane and open the window and speak to you. During Christmas you will come down to us with the angels and then we'll live again together as a family and then we'll all die together, Mummy, you, Christopher, and I.

Death and how to explain it

According to Kübler-Ross (1969), one can discern a 'grief cycle' representing how people cope with death. This cycle is evident for not only the person dying but also the people affected by the death. Initial paralysis at hearing the bad news results in shock, which is followed by denial. Often people become angry and then they try to bargain. After the realization that bargaining is futile, depression sets in; this might be followed by a stage in which the person looks for realistic solutions to the problem and the final stage is the acceptance stage in which the person accepts what is happening and moves forward. This chapter is an account of how Toto coped with the death of her father from cancer. The question asked is how do young children cope with loss and the ultimate loss, namely death? Having learned from her father about happiness, sadness, fear and anger, this chapter is an account of the experience of death by Toto, who lived through her father's illness from just before her fifth birthday to his death from brain cancer just before her sixth birthday. Has her father equipped her to cope with his loss at this very young age?

Hospitalization

Sunday, the 16th of April, Daddy is feeling unwell. Toto (4 years 11 months) and her brother Christopher (1 year 6 months) are excited because we all go to hospital. There Daddy is diagnosed as having an inoperable brain tumour. Daddy has to stay in hospital. We go home and bring him pyjamas and toothbrush, help him to get undressed, share his dinner, and go home. No evening read. Daddy is in hospital. The next morning Toto is told by her mother that Daddy is going to die.

According to Kübler-Ross (1969), there are several stages of coping with death: the first one is the denial of death.

Denial of the coming death

The progression of the cancer is rapid, and with his double vision and beginning aphasia, Daddy cannot read any more to Toto. Toto comments: 'Daddy can't read any more to me, so I read to him.' She lies beside him on the hospital bed and 'reads' her story books by heart. Daddy is lying in hospital as a private patient, but the nurses don't have any time to help him wash or shave. Christopher, Mummy and Toto help Daddy to get into the shower and while the children wash his feet with lots of soap, Mummy washes the rest of his body. We all get wet. It is good fun to help Daddy. Toto draws a picture for Daddy, which we stick to the hospital wall, opposite his bed. It shows Daddy at home. Daddy fills the space of the house, smiling. Only the house door is black. Toto is hopeful that he will get better.

Although there is in the back of her mind the worry that he might not, and that we will have to live without Daddy: another picture she draws for the hospital wall depicts only three people, Mummy, Christopher and Toto, under the rainbow.

Toto realizes that she is powerless in the face of death. During the following months, Toto attempts again and again to deny the illness. Radiation treatment begins and after one week Daddy comes back home for a weekend. He cannot walk any more and his speech and voice are impaired. Toto insists: 'My Daddy is not here.'

Later we all (a number of friends have come) sit around the dining room table and eat. Daddy eats with his left hand because the right one is increasingly paralysed. Toto sits on her Daddy's lap. Both are happy. He is home, after all.

Having learned to talk about emotions with her Daddy, she now thinks it is 'normal' to talk about emotions with him, even though it concerns talk about his death. Toto explains death and life after death to her Daddy. After three weeks of radiation therapy Daddy comes home, permanently. Toto sits on his bed showing him 'Mary and Baby Jesus' and telling him about paradise:

> It is very nice there. And we can fly up in the plane and open the window and speak to you. During Christmas you will come down to us with the angels and then we'll live again together as a family and then we'll all die together, Mummy, you, Christopher, and I.

In the coming weeks, Toto 'helps' Daddy by feeding him when he cannot hold his fork any more, or by moving his limbs when they get more and more paralysed. She thinks that no matter what, she will always be able to move his limbs for him. When he sits in the wheelchair and cannot hold his feet up so that they get stuck under the wheels, she carries the feet while I move the chair. When her father cannot open his eyes any more, she lifts his eyelids with her fingertips, asking him to look at her. When she wants to cuddle him, she places his arm around her waist. She even translates for him when he cannot make himself understood. For example, when he throws on the floor some flowers which are arranged on the windowsill beside his bed and I angrily tell him that I won't buy any flowers for him any more, Toto says: 'But Mummy, he doesn't like the colour!' At about that same time, she draws a picture of Mummy and Christopher standing outside our house and comments: 'I am inside the house taking care of Daddy.'

Another day on which there is nobody who can take care of Daddy while I go shopping, I ask Toto whether she might watch him while I quickly run out with Christopher to do some errands. When I come back, Toto says: 'I fed Daddy a whole banana.' Mother responds: 'Are you sure, Toto – he can't swallow any more and might choke.' At the time of his complete paralysis, she walks unasked into his room and comes out saying, 'He ate an apple' – she even asks me eventually to buy her a 'magician's stick', a baton she saw in a shop window; it had small stars floating in a viscous liquid inside. Toto said: 'I need it to make Daddy healthy again.' She stands beside the bed with the stick and doesn't know any more what to say. She slowly seems to grasp the fact that even she cannot make Daddy healthy again.

She starts to draw pictures of Daddy as an angel. In November she draws herself and Daddy in heaven, and Mummy and Christopher are on earth. Heaven and earth are connected through steps and framed by a rainbow. Toto walks up the steps and 'visits Daddy in heaven'.

As the effect of the brain tumour spreads through his body, Daddy seems to become more detached from earth. One of her pictures shows him floating in a coffin-like shape in the air while Toto, Christopher and Mummy stand outside our house, smiling.

Another picture shows him as a black figure floating among flowers.

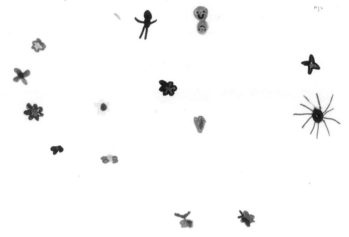

Death and life after death

After having lived with the progression of the illness, in which his right side becomes completely paralysed and his eyes are rarely open and only small pieces of food can be swallowed (which Toto gives to him) and the pain increases (which Toto tries to control by massaging his legs, arms and forehead with oil), her ideas about death change. Dead people, according to her, are different from angels: 'Angels open in the mornings the eyes of the dead people and so they [the dead] are awake. And angels cook for the dead people.'

Also her idea of how we will be able to communicate with Daddy, who cannot see any more and is completely paralysed and is being nourished through a tube, changes. In order to talk to Daddy, now, one has to go to church: 'We'll go to church and then we can talk to Daddy.'

Death

The illness progresses, with more sleepiness and more epileptic seizures and in the end complete stillness. At the time of his death, Toto lies beside her Daddy in bed, Christopher sits on his bed, and I hold his hand. His last breath and he is dead. Toto wants to help to get him dressed. 'His trousers are so loose.' 'The socks are difficult to pull over his feet.' 'And what about shoes.' Toto is told her Daddy is dead. But she insists: 'Daddy is only half dead.' 'Daddy is cold.' Toto touches him before he is carried out of our house.

The funeral

We will have a last feast for Daddy, in which children are the main guests and coloured balloons filled with gas float up to heaven where Daddy now lives. We give him a few last gifts before the coffin lid is sealed, including chocolate from Christopher, a boat folded out of golden paper from Toto, and two little toy monkeys to play with. 'Will they throw him in this hole?' No, the men are careful. The children stick colourful bouquets of flowers all around the grave and throw some in the grave so that 'it's nice down there for Daddy.' We sing a song of the rainbow, which is depicted in many of Toto's drawings.

At that stage, Toto tries to understand death. 'Daddy is dead.' And again and again the question: 'Why did our Daddy have to die?' Answer from Toto: 'He ate something bad and then he did not go to the doctor when he had headaches.'

Despite her rationalization, that Daddy had omitted something, such as going to the doctor, she is afraid that her Mummy is also going to die. She doesn't want me to leave the house and if I have to leave, she stays in by the telephone just in case something happens to me.

Passage to heaven

Acceptance of the inevitable and Toto talks about Daddy's passage to heaven.

One Sunday morning when her father was still alive, Toto talks about Daddy's passage to heaven.

> Daddy's heart goes up first to heaven in the sky and then his body is going up and then heart and body are going together again. After body and heart are together again he gets small white bits coming out of the arms, but his arms are still there. Angels are very nice. Angels and Daddy are going to wait till another person dies and then this person is getting as well an angel. In heaven Daddy is friends with the angels. Daddy looks down onto me and he is still my Daddy. I come as well soon to heaven after I have lived because I must die as well.

Ten days after his death Toto makes up the following poem in German:

Daddy liegt im Sarg schon fein ist auch
bald ein Engelein.

Daddy ist bestreut mit gelb, blau, rosa und grünen Blumen und
Tannenzweigen.

Kommen alle fein in Pracht durch die
finstere schwarze Nacht.

(Daddy lies in the coffin nice and fine, will be soon a little angel.
Daddy is sprinkled with yellow, blue, rose and green flowers and
with fir branches. Everybody is coming in splendour through the
gloomy black night.)

One evening, after her father has been dead for eight months, Toto
talks again about the road to heaven. But now she sees it in a more
detached way. She does not talk about other people's or her own
death any more. Sitting in the bathtub Toto explains:

Toto: He was first in a glass cage. Once he reached heaven his
           wings began to grow. They are not fully grown yet.
Mother: How long will it be until they are fully grown?
Toto: Perhaps a week or two.

Practical ideas about life after death:

Two days after Daddy's death, Toto draws a picture showing 'Daddy
and his angel friend and God.' Angels have angel friends so that they
are not lonely.

   Daddy is depicted without spectacles because 'angels have no spectacles'. In heaven one finds colourful houses, windows with curtains
and swings or hammocks. It snows in heaven, black snowflakes.

   And one celebrates feasts like Christmas and Easter, as a dancing
Easter bunny in heaven illustrates. One morning Toto recounts:

'Daddy is taking care of angel children, playing with them.' However, life in heaven is not only colourful like the rainbow. Another morning Toto tells us: 'The angel children were fighting and Daddy made peace between them.'

Cognitive development and changing ideas about death and life after death

Toto says at the dinner table after her father has been dead four months: 'God is air.'

Mother: Why?
Toto: Because He lives in heaven.
Mother: Angels are then also air?
Toto: No, they were people before, and after they died they flew up to Him.

'God is air' – in other words, 'not really existing'. Angels, specifically Daddy, are real – they do exist, because they were people before. In her pictures, Toto draws us all the same. For example, in her picture 'Angels on Earth Having a Party in the Woods by a Stone,' she depicts all of us with wings and no arms. Christopher, not Daddy, is depicted walking down the steps from heaven.

Two months later, Daddy is distinguished from us: he is now an angel with wings, whereas Toto, Christopher and Mummy are drawn with small wings as well as arms.

An important day

It is Daddy's birthday. Toto recounts when I wake her up in the morning of the 14th:

Toto: Daddy was on a bicycle with only one wheel and he was cycling on water. I had a string which was attached to the

wheel and I could pull him with that string back to me
when I wanted to.

Mother: Did you do it?
Toto: Yes.

Toto is thinking of our puppy dog Muni, whose leash extends to eight
metres but she can be pulled back when necessary.

At the breakfast table Christopher wants to give Daddy chocolate:
'No, a cake, a birthday cake!' Mother: 'Why don't you sing a song for
Daddy?' Toto starts to sing 'Happy Birthday', but then stops. Toto
doesn't sing any more. She says: 'We have to have a surprise for him.'
It is time to leave for school. Toto, on the way: 'Mummy, are you
going to buy a surprise for us today, a small one?' Toto wants to
celebrate Daddy's birthday, not by eating birthday cake but by her
and her brother receiving a surprise, not her father. In the evening, we
bake a chocolate cake, light a candle for Daddy, and eat the cake with
some friends.

Visits to the grave and the practicalities of it

Toto asks one day why we should go to the graveyard to see Daddy.
'We could sit him in a corner of the garden, and then we would
always see him.' When Toto leaves the grave, she always says:
'Goodbye Daddy,' bowing in front of the grave, 'see you next week.'

After another month Toto's ideas about Daddy change from
Daddy as a person who is living in heaven to Daddy as a 'person'
living in Toto's heart.

Toto says: 'You see,' reaching in the air around her, 'Daddy is
always with us; you just cannot see him. He is always in *my* heart.'

As time passes visits to the grave change. The grave is decorated
with new plants and the children do not say 'goodbye' any more.
They comment: 'They are nice colourful flowers for Daddy's grave.'

The first big event after Daddy's death

Toto's first school day arrives. She cries a little and says that she is sad
that Daddy isn't with us. The day after her first school day, we go to
visit Daddy's grave.

Mother: Did you tell Daddy about your first day in school?
Toto: I do not have to tell him, he saw it!

In one picture of her coming home from school, she expresses her slow detachment from her father – one sees only his hand. Toto explains: 'Daddy is waving from the roof. We pretend he is still alive.'

Ten months later

After ten months have passed since his death, although we still talk about Daddy, he is, at least in Toto's mind, not with us any more. She only occasionally recounts dreams about us all, including the dog Muni-Spot, sitting in heaven and enjoying each other's company. In her pictures she more often depicts three figures. For example, there is a picture of Mummy-mouse, Toto-mouse, and Christopher-mouse eating cheese with holes. Toto is getting accustomed to a life without Daddy. Only sometimes, she dreams it isn't true and then she draws a picture of 'Mummy-clown and Daddy-clown.'

Conclusion

Many 'important' milestones have been achieved since Toto's first day of school, but still the cycle of grieving is repeated. It seems that there will never be complete acceptance of death, although coping with the death of Daddy has prepared Toto to cope with other losses. Having become accustomed to live her life without Daddy, she mentions from time to time positive aspects of living the life she lives without her Daddy. Sometimes, though, she worries: 'Will I forget him?'

13 Conclusion

Toto under a walnut tree: some of them are out of reach, others she catches and some of them fall on her head.

What have we learned about the development of emotionally intelligent behaviour in the context of the first few years of life? Although Toto's opportunity for learning from her father was cut short by his death, the chapters of the case study illustrate his influence on her emotional development. In the preceding chapters we were able to get an insight into how daily life might contribute to the development of emotional functioning in various domains, which are considered to be part of a concept of EI.

If we accept that emotional intelligence can be subsumed under the following five characteristics (Goleman 1995), an emotionally mature person should demonstrate: 'managing one's emotions', in terms of being able to cope with fear, anger, sadness or happiness; 'self-awareness', which includes the ability to recognize and identify one's emotions; 'self-motivation', which includes emotional control and the ability to work towards goals with the expectations that one succeeds; 'empathy', which includes the ability to recognize emotions and behave sensitively towards others; and lastly being able to 'negotiate relationships', including the ability to handle conflict, find constructive solutions to conflict and generally be able to have and maintain good relationships with others.

The case study illustrates important principles leading to the socialization of emotional intelligence. Teaching about emotions in a social context by labelling emotions occurs in the first few days of life. However, not all emotions are introduced at the same time. Based on the audio diaries, it becomes apparent that emotional labels for happiness and sadness are introduced before fear is labelled. We can follow the process from the first few weeks of life to the time when Toto asserts her independence as a toddler. As she grows more mature so her father gives her more responsibilities for her actions and her moral obligations towards others. Even as a 2 year old, she learns that she needs to behave in such a way that others do not get hurt. Hence, the definition of emotional intelligence, which includes the ability to appraise another's emotional state as well as manage one's own emotions (Mayer et al. 2008), is relevant here, in that we can follow the development of the immature infant behaviour to the increasingly responsible behaviour of the toddler. In the context of the development of managing one's emotions, Toto learns how to deal with conflict by observing how her father copes with various difficult situations or discusses with her how she might be able to cope with her own problems. For example, once Toto is old enough and capable of teasing herself, she has to learn how to negotiate the fine line between what is acceptable teasing behaviour and what is unacceptable or naughty behaviour.

Empathy is another important aspect of emotional intelligence. In the case study we learn that the father distinguishes between thoughts and feelings and between pretend and real emotions. Toto's capacity for empathy is demonstrated during the last phase of her father's life. Here she makes up angel friends for him so that he would not feel lonely in heaven; she reassures her father by telling him that life in heaven is enjoyable and that he could come down to earth and visit over Christmas. There will be a happy ending when we all live with him in heaven.

Growing self-awareness in relation to emotional context is discussed in terms of emotional intelligence being related to the differentiation of the self, the 'I' from the other 'you'; furthermore thoughts or cognitions are differentiated from emotions. Talking about feelings in general in contrast to talking about thoughts in general occurred very rarely at an early age. Rather the father talks about specific emotion indicators, such as a 'smile' or a 'cry'. This is followed by talking about happiness, sadness, fear or anger during specific emotional events. In contrast, the father mentions 'feelings' as abstract concepts only in passing at this early stage of development.

Following the child's journey mainly through her father's eyes, we encounter the father's rhetorical use of language. This illustrates the development of the father's perception of the increased sophistication of his daughter. The development of Toto in terms of her ability and willingness to comply with requests, such as not to eat dirt from the floor, changes over time. Additionally, the differentiation of the self from the other is discussed in the context of an analysis of the rhetoric her father uses when she is on the changing table. In order to establish the development of Toto's ability to distinguish the self 'I' from the other 'you', her father's use of 'I' and 'you' was analysed as a percentage of his utterances to the baby while changing her from 1 to 15 months of age. There was a significant positive correlation between the mean frequency of using 'I' as a percentage of the text analysed and the age of the baby. As the baby grew older so there was more use of 'I', indicating that Toto's father referred more often to himself as his daughter developed from 1 to 15 months. In contrast there was no significant correlation between age and use of 'you'. Hence, the father's use of 'you' did not change over time. However comparing the use of 'I' with the use of 'you', the 'you' is used significantly more often at all ages. The 'I' was used a mean percentage of 1.13 times per conversation while speaking to his daughter whereas 'you' was used with a mean percentage of 6.12 times per conversation, indicating that Toto's father addressed his daughter more often than he referred to himself in talking to her.

Emotional self-awareness is an ability which includes recognizing, naming and understanding the cause of emotions experienced (Salovey and Mayer 1990). We learn how the baby is taught about emotional self-awareness by tracing the development of teasing from the time that Toto gets teased to the time that she teases her father. The analysis of teasing demonstrates that teasing can be a pleasant experience and is the basis for the child to become able to interact in her environment in an emotionally mature way. A child, who is able not only to identify feeling 'bad' but also to say that he or she is angry, hurt, jealous, sad or scared in various contexts, shows emotional intelligence by being able to differentiate finely between different emotions. The same is true for positive emotions. The analysis of teasing behaviours and reactions to teasing permits an analysis of the developmental progress of emotional intelligence. In infancy, some forms of play, such as playing peek-a-boo, create tension between participants by incorporating some form of ambiguity. This tension created by the ambiguity of the interaction may elicit a positive response, such as laughter, from the baby. The infant can, however, also perceive teasing negatively, and hence create an aversive reaction in the child. Creating tension in play relates to the concept of teasing, defined as an act that is directed to achieve affective consequences for the target of the action (Keltner et al. 2001).

Emotional differentiation, namely that there are many shades of happiness, is introduced when discussing the functions of smiles. The child learns not only that when smiling she feels better but also that there are degrees of happiness, depending on the intensity of the emotion experienced. Furthermore, positive emotions are differentiated in various ways by talking about the experience of emotions, to talking about Toto's well-being specifically, to talking about degrees of happiness elicited in various situations.

Self-motivation in terms of setting goals and working towards them is illustrated in Toto's ability to deal with her father's dying and death. Toto first tried to find ways to make Daddy 'better' or healthy. She had to accept daily challenges to accomplish this goal, for example by lifting his legs when they got paralysed or putting his arms around her waist when she wanted a cuddle and he could not move them any more, and finally using a magic wand to make him healthy again. Even in the light of defeat she set herself new goals and in the end started accepting the inevitable.

In sum, the validity of the concept of emotional intelligence or tests of emotional intelligence, are disputed by some as being popular, untested or untestable, which would not stand up to the scrutiny of scientific investigation. Others embrace the idea as the increasing number of programmes applied in schools to teach emotional intelligence bear witness to. It is argued in this book, that although it is clear that the concept of EI still needs to be tested rigorously in various contexts, the foundations for emotionally intelligent behaviours are laid down from the first days of life.

14 Emotional intelligence for parents

WEBSITES

A survey of results of websites on EI in Google resulted in 2,250,000 returns in January 2011. Hence EI is becoming more popular. Below are some websites which might be of interest for parents and their children.

KidSource
www.kidsource.com/kidsource/content4/emot.intel.html

On this website, Joshua Freedman states:

> As a parent, you should care about EQ [emotional intelligence] because your child is growing up in a complicated, changing world – one where her experiences will be very different from your own. Faced with new situations, we can not simply pull one of our parent's solutions from our bag of tricks – we must be able to invent solutions.
>
> You want to be sure that those solutions help her live as a whole and healthy human being. And the most essential tool we have to accomplish that goal is our ability to sense and communicate emotions.
>
> In addition, all other areas of learning and growth hinge on emotional intelligence. Our emotional brain is the part where we decide what to pay attention to, the place where long term memory is stored, and the area where we set priorities. As Plato wrote, '**All learning has an emotional base.**'

Headroom
www.headroom.net.au/Content.aspx?p=231

This website asks:

Who or what are 'emotionally intelligent' parents and how can they help?

These parents have the ability to distinguish between feelings. They also show empathy for their children and model how to manage feelings in relationships.

There is evidence that shows these parents can make a difference for their children. These parents have children who:

- are more affectionate
- are less tense around their parents
- are better at handling their feelings
- are more effective at calming themselves
- get upset less often
- are more popular with their peers
- are rated as more socially skilled by their teachers
- have longer attention spans and so are more effective learners

Parenting the at risk child
www.parentingtheatriskchild.com/store/emotional_
intelligence.html

On this website the following promises are made:

> The Parent's Store is your source of books and other resources for preventive parenting. Our goal is to help you parent now to prevent later difficulties with antisocial behavior, addiction and ADHD. The earlier you begin the techniques of prevention we recommend, the greater your chances of complete prevention will be. **It is our mission to provide you with the tools you need to parent your at risk child**.
>
> At risk children are at risk in part, because they have a hard time with emotional intelligence. They may be intellectually bright but at risk children may be 'learning disabled' when it comes to emotional intelligence.

Rainbow Planet Connection
www.rainbowplanetconnection.com/

This website states:

> We offer a unique range of fun, creative educational courses and resources to support the development of SOCIAL AND EMOTIONAL WELL-BEING in children and families.

Child parenting about.com
www.childparenting.about.com/od/socialdevelopment/a/
teach_empathy_and_emotional_intelligence.htm

This website suggests:

> There are many reasons why parents should consider teaching empathy and nurturing emotional intelligence in their kids. In basic terms, empathy is the ability to be able to put oneself in someone else's shoes and understand that person's emotions and feelings.

Increase your EQ
www.increaseyoureq.com/resources-eq.php

This website lists a number of emotional intelligence websites including the following:

The EI consortium
www.eiconsortium.org

The consortium, led by Daniel Goleman, includes experts in emotional intelligence, such as Peter Salovey, Reuven Bar-On and Richard Boyatzis. Here you will find the latest research and information related to emotional intelligence in the workplace.

Emotional intelligence information
www.unh.edu/emotional_intelligence

This is John D. Mayer's site, which contains a wealth of information on emotional intelligence, including information on cognition, affect and mood measurements.

Bar-On Model of Social-Emotional Intelligence
www.reuvenbaron.org

This is the website of Reuven Bar-On, University of Texas Medical Branch.

6 Seconds
www.6seconds.org

A non-profit, emotional intelligence network dedicated to teaching emotional intelligence skills in schools, organizations and communities around the world. An interesting site for educators, parents and counsellors, it includes an EQ store as well and has a number of online resources, including research and training materials.

Institute of HeartMath
www.heartmath.org

This is an innovative non-profit, research and education organization whose mission is to facilitate people in finding the balance between mind and heart in life's decisions. The institute has developed the HeartMath System: a set of practical techniques and technologies to help people transmute stress and negative emotions in the moment, improve performance and enrich the quality of life.

CASEL
www.casel.org

The Collaborative for Academic, Social, and Emotional Learning (CASEL), Department of Psychology, University of Illinois, Chicago. Its mission is to 'enhance children's success in school and life by promoting coordinated, evidence-based social, emotional, and academic learning as an essential part of education from preschool through high school.'

BOOKS

Here is a selection of book titles on emotional intelligence for carers in alphabetical order: parents need to judge for themselves which of these books might be helpful.

Bahman, S., and Maffini, H. (2008) *Developing Children's Emotional Intelligence*. New York: Continuum Education.

Bar-On, R., and Parker, J.D.A. (eds) (2000) *The Handbook of Emotional Intelligence: Theory, Development, Assessment, and Application at Home, School and in the Workplace*. San Francisco, CA: Jossey-Bass.

Blaine, K.C. (2011) *The Go-to Mom's Parents' Guide to Emotion Coaching Young Children*. San Francisco, CA: Jossey-Bass.

Bradberry, T., and Greaves, J. (2009) *Emotional Intelligence 2.0*. San Diego, CA: Talent Smart.

Elias, M.J., Tobias, S.E., and Friedlander, B.S. (2000) *Raising Emotionally Intelligent Teenagers: Parenting with Love, Laughter, and Limits*. New York: Harmony.

Elias, M.J., Tobias, S.E., Friedlander, B.S., and Goleman, D. (2000) *Emotionally Intelligent Parenting: How to Raise a Self-Disciplined, Responsible, Socially Skilled Child*. New York: Three Rivers Press.

Glennon, W. (2000) *200 Ways to Raise a Boy's Emotional Intelligence: An Indispensable Guide for Parents, Teachers and Other Concerned Caregivers*. Berkeley, CA: Conari.

Gottman, J., and DeClaire, J. (1997) *Raising an Emotionally Intelligent Child: The Heart of Parenting*. New York: Simon & Schuster.

Greenspan, S.I., and Lewis, N. (1999) *Building Healthy Minds: The Six Experiences that Create Intelligence and Emotional Growth in Babies and Young Children*. Cambridge, MA: Perseus.

Lantieri, L., and Goleman, D. (2008) *Building Emotional Intelligence: Techniques to Cultivate Inner Strength in Children*. Boulder, CO: Sounds True.

Nagy, A., and Nagy, G. (1999) *How to Raise Your Child's Emotional Intelligence: 101 Ways to Bring Out the Best in Your Children and Yourself*. Lakewood, CO: Heartfelt

Neihart, M., Reis, S.M., Robinson, N.M., and Moon, S.M. (2001) *Social and Emotional Development of Gifted Children: What Do We Know?* Washington, DC: National Association for Gifted Children.

Rudd, B. (2009) *Help Your Child Develop Emotional Literacy: The Parents' Guide to Happy Children*. New York: Continuum International.

Shapiro, L.E. (1998) *How to Raise a Child with a High EQ: A Parents' Guide to Emotional Intelligence*. New York: Harper Paperbacks.

Schiller, P.B. (2009) *Seven Skills for School Success: Activities to Develop Social and Emotional Intelligence in Young Children*. Beltsville, MD: Gryphon House.

Windell, J. (1999) *Six Steps to an Emotionally Intelligent Teenager: Teaching Social Skills to Your Teen*. New York: Wiley.

References

Acredolo, L., and Goodwyn, S. (1988) Symbolic gesturing in normal infants. *Child Development*, 59: 450–466.

Ambrose, A. (1963) The age and onset of ambivalence in early infancy: Indications from the study of laughing. *Journal of Child Psychology and Psychiatry*, 4: 167–181.

Astington, J.W., and Jenkins, J.M. (1999) A longitudinal study of the relations between language and theory-of-mind development. *Developmental Psychology*, 5: 1311–1320.

Austin, E.J., Saklofske, D.H., and Egan, V. (2005) Personality, well-being and health correlates of trait emotional intelligence. *Personality and Individual Differences*, 38: 547–558.

Austin, E.J., Farrelly, D., Black, C., and Moore, H. (2007) Emotional intelligence, Machiavellianism and emotional manipulation: Does EI have a dark side? *Personality and Individual Differences*, 43: 179–189.

Bachorowski, J-A. (1999) Vocal expression and perception of emotion. *Current Directions in Psychological Science*, 8: 53–57.

Bachorowski, J-A., and Owren, M.J. (2002) The role of vocal acoustics in emotional intelligence. In L.F. Barrett and P. Salovey (eds) *The Wisdom of Feelings: Processes Underlying Emotional Intelligence* (pp. 11–36). New York: Guilford.

Bamber, M.R. (2006) *CBT for Occupational Stress in Health Professionals: Introducing a Schema-based Approach.* New York: Routledge.

Banse, R., and Scherer, K.R. (1996) Acoustic profiles in vocal emotion expression. *Journal of Personality and Social Psychology*, 70: 614–636.

Bar-On, R. (1997) *The Bar-On Emotional Quotient Inventory (EQ-i): A Test of Emotional Intelligence.* Toronto: Multi-Health Systems.

Bar-On, R. (2002) *The Bar-On Emotional Quotient Inventory: Short Technical Manual.* Toronto: Multi-Health Systems.

Bar-On, R. (2004) The Bar-On Emotional Quotient Inventory (EQ-i): Rationale, description, and summary of psychometric properties. In G. Geher (ed.) *Measuring Emotional Intelligence: Common Ground and Controversy* (pp. 111–142). Hauppauge, NY: Nova Science Publishers.

Baron-Cohen, S., Jolliffe, T., Mortimore, C., and Robertson, M. (1997) Another advanced test of theory of mind: Evidence from very high functioning adults with autism or Asperger syndrome. *Journal of Child Psychology and Psychiatry*, 38: 813–822.

Bates, E., Camaioni, L., and Volterra, V. (1975) The acquisition of performatives prior to speech. *Merrill Palmer Quarterly*, 21: 205–226.

Beaumont, S.L., and Bloom, K. (1993) Adults' attributions of intentionality to vocalizing infants. *First Language*, 13: 235–247.

Beebe, B., Badalamenti, A., Jaffe, J., Marquette, L., Helbraun, E., Andrews, H., and Ellman, L. (2008) Distressed mothers and their infants use less efficient timing mechanisms in creating visual expectancies. *Journal of Linguistic Research*, 37: 293–307.

Bell, S.M., and Ainsworth, M.D.S. (1972) Infant crying and maternal responsiveness. *Child Development*, 43: 1171–1190.

Belsky, J., Fish, M., and Isabella, R. (1991) Continuity and discontinuity in infant negative and positive emotionality: Family antecedents and attachment consequences. *Developmental Psychology*, 27: 421–431.

Bergin, C. (1987) Prosocial development in toddlers: The patterning of mother–infant interactions. In M.E. Ford and D.H. Ford (eds) *Humans as Self-constructing Living Systems: Putting the Framework to Work* (pp. 121–143). Hillsdale, NJ: Lawrence Erlbaum Associates.

Bergin, C., and Bergin, D.A. (1999) Classroom discipline that promotes self-control. *Journal of Applied Developmental Psychology*, 20: 189–206.

Biber, D., Johansson, S., Leech, G., Conrad, S., and Finnegan, E. (1999) *Longman Grammar of Spoken and Written English*. London: Longman.

Blake, J., and Fink, R. (1987) Sound-meaning correspondences in babbling. *Journal of Child Language*, 14: 229–253.

Bloom, L. (1973) *One Word at a Time*. The Hague: Mouton.

Bloom, L. (1998) Language development and emotional expression. *Paediatrics*, 102: 1272–1277.

Bloom, P., and German, T.P. (2000) Two reasons to abandon the false belief task as a test of theory of mind. *Cognition*, 77: B25–B31.

Bornstein, M.H., and Arterberry, M.E. (2003) Recognition, discrimination and categorization of smiling by 5-month-old infants. *Developmental Science*, 6: 585–599.

Brackett, M.A., and Geher, G. (2006) Measuring emotional intelligence: Paradigmatic diversity and common ground. In J. Ciarrochi, J.P. Forgas and J.D. Mayer (eds) *Emotional Intelligence and Everyday Life*, 2nd edn (pp. 27–50). New York: Psychology Press.

Brackett, M.A., Mayer, J.D., and Waner, R.M. (2004) Emotional intelligence and its relation to everyday behaviour. *Personality and Individual Differences*, 36: 1387–1402.

Brackett, M.A., Rivers, S.E., Shiffman, S., Lerner, N., and Salovey, P. (2006) Relating emotional abilities to social functioning: A comparison of self report and performance measures of emotional intelligence. *Journal of Personality and Social Psychology*, 91: 780–795.

Brannick, M.T., Wahi, M.M., Arce, M., Johnson, H.A., Nazian, S., and Goldin, S.B. (2009) Comparison of trait and ability measures of emotional intelligence in medical students. *Medical Education*, 43: 1062–1068.

Broerse, J., and Elias, G. (1994) Changes in the content and timing of mothers' talk to infants. *British Journal of Developmental Psychology*, 12: 131–145.

Brown, R. (1977) Introduction. In C.E. Snow and C.A. Ferguson (eds) *Talking to Children: Language Input and Acquisition* (pp. 1–27). Cambridge: Cambridge University Press.

Bruner, J. (1982) The organization of action and the nature of adult–infant transaction. In M. von Cranach and R. Harré (eds) *The Analysis of Action* (pp. 313–327). New York: Cambridge University Press.

Buck, R. (1993) Emotional communication, emotional competence, and physical illness. In J. Pennebaker and H. Traue (eds) *Emotional Expressiveness, Inhibition, and Health* (pp. 32–56). Seattle, WA: Hogrefe & Huber.

Bulmer-Smith, K., Profetto-McGrath, J., and Cummings, G.G. (2009) Emotional intelligence and nursing: An integrative literature review. *International Journal of Nursing Studies*, 46: 1624–1636.

Cabrera, N.J., Shannon, J.D., and Tamis-LeMonda, C. (2007) Fathers' influence on their children's cognitive and emotional development: From toddlers to pre-K. *Applied Developmental Science*, 11: 208–213.

Campos, J.J., Mumme, D.L., Kermoian, R., and Campos, R.G. (1994) A functionalist perspective on the nature of emotion. In N. Fox (ed.) *The Development of Emotion Regulation: Biological and Behavioral Considerations. Monographs of the Society for Research in Child Development*, 59 (2–3, no. 240); 284–303.

Camras, L.A. (2000) Surprise! Facial expressions can be coordinative motor structures. In M. Lewis and I. Granic (eds) *Emotion, Development, and Self-organization* (pp. 100–124). New York: Cambridge University Press.

Camras, L.A., and Allison, K. (1985) Children's understanding of emotional facial expressions and verbal labels. *Journal of Nonverbal Behavior*, 9: 84–94.

Carroll, J.B. (1993) *Human Cognitive Abilities*. Cambridge: Cambridge University Press.

Chang, E.C., Maydeu-Olivares, A., and D'Zurilla, T.J. (1997) Optimism and pessimism as partially independent constructs: Relations to positive and negative affectivity and psychological well-being. *Personality and Individual Differences*, 23: 433–440.

Cherniss, C. (2004) Intelligence, Emotional. In C.D. Spielberger (ed.) *Encyclopedia of Applied Psychology*, vol. 2 (pp. 315–319). Amsterdam: Elsevier.

Cherry, L.J. (1976) Interactive strategies in language development: A sociocognitive model. Paper presented at the Conference on Language, Children, and Society, Ohio State University, April.

Chorpita, B.F., and Barlow, D.H. (1998) The development of anxiety: The role of control in the early environment. *Psychological Bulletin*, 124: 3–21.

Ciarrochi, J., Chan, A., and Caputi, P. (2000) A critical evaluation of the emotional intelligence construct. *Personality and Individual Differences*, 28: 539–561.

Ciarrochi, J., Deane, F.P., and Anderson, S. (2002) Emotional intelligence moderates the relationship between stress and mental health. *Personality and Individual Differences*, 32: 197–209.

Cicchetti, D., Rogosch, F.A., and Toth, S.L. (1998) Maternal depressive disorder and contextual risk: Contributions to the development of attachment insecurity and behavior problems in toddlerhood. *Development and Psychopathology*, 10: 283–300.

Cohen, N.J. (2003) Overlap of communication impairments and social-emotional problems in infants. *Newsletter of the Infant Mental Health Promotion Project*, 37: 1–3.

Cooper, R.P., Abraham, J., Berman, S., and Staska, M. (1997) The development of infant's preference for motherese. *Infant Behavior and Development*, 20: 477–488.

Cournoyer, M., and Trudel, M. (1991) Behavioral correlates of self-control at 33 months. *Infant Behavior and Development*, 14: 497–503.

Cranley, M.S. (1981) Development of a tool for the measurement of maternal attachment during pregnancy. *Nursing Research*, 30: 281–284.

Crockenberg, S.C., and Leerkes, E.M. (2004) Infant and maternal behaviors regulate infant reactivity to novelty at 6 months. *Developmental Psychology*, 40: 1123–1132.

Darwin, C. (1872) *The Expression of the Emotions in Man and Animals*. London: William Pickering.

Day, A.L., Therrien, D.L., and Carroll, S.A. (2005) Predicting psychological health: Assessing the incremental validity of emotional intelligence beyond personality, type A behaviour, and daily hassles. *European Journal of Personality*, 19: 519–536.

Denham, S.A., Mitchell-Copeland, J., Strandberg, K., Auerbach, S., and Blair, K. (1997) Parental contributions to preschoolers' emotional competence: Direct and indirect effects. *Motivation and Emotion*, 21: 65–86.

Denham, S.A., Zoller, D., and Couchoud, E.A. (1994) Socialization of preschoolers' emotion understanding. *Developmental Psychology*, 30: 928–936.

de Raad, B. (2005) The trait-coverage of emotional intelligence. *Personality and Individual Differences*, 38: 673–687.

de Waal, F.B.M. (1996) *Good Natured: The Origins of Right and Wrong in Humans and Other Animals*. Cambridge, MA: Harvard University Press.

de Waal, F.B.M. (2008) Putting the altruism back into altruism: The evolution of empathy. *Annual Review of Psychology*, 59: 279–300.

Dimberg, U., and Thunberg, M. (1998) Rapid facial reactions to emotional facial expressions. *Scandinavian Journal of Psychology*, 39: 39–45.

Dissanayake, C., and Macintosh, K. (2003) Mind reading and social functioning in children with autistic disorder and Asperger's disorder. In B. Repacholi and V. Slaughter (eds) *Individual Differences in Theory of Mind: Implications for Typical and Atypical Development*. New York: Psychology Press.

D'Odorico, L., and France, E. (1991) Selective production of vocalization types in different communication contexts. *Journal of Child Language*, 18: 475–499.

Dondi, M., Simion, F., and Caltran, G. (1999) Can newborns discriminate between their own cry and the cry of another newborn infant? *Developmental Psychology*, 35: 418–426.

Dumas, J.E., Lemay, P., and Dauwalder, J. (2001) Dynamic analyses of mother–child interactions in functional and dysfunctional dyads: A synergetic approach. *Journal of Abnormal Child Psychology*, 29: 317–329.

Dunn, L.M., and Dunn, L.M. (1997) *Peabody Picture Vocabulary Test*, 3rd edn. Circle Pines, MN: American Guidance Service.

Durand, K., Gallay, M., Seigneuric, A., Robichon, F., and Baudouin, J.Y. (2007) The development of facial emotion recognition: The role of configural information. *Journal of Experimental Child Psychology*, 97: 14–27.

Durbin, C.E. (2010) Validity of young children's self-reports of their emotion in response to structured laboratory tasks. *Emotion*, 10: 519–535.

Eder, D. (1991) The role of teasing in adolescent peer group culture. *Sociological Studies of Child Development*, 2: 181–197.

Eisenberg, A. (1986) Teasing: Verbal play in two Mexicano homes. In B.B. Schieffelin and E. Ochs (eds) *Language Socialization across Cultures* (pp. 182–198). Cambridge: Cambridge University Press.

Eisenberg, N. (2000) Emotion, regulation, and moral development. *Annual Review of Psychology*, 51: 665–697.

Eisenberg, N., Cumberland, A., and Spinrad, T.L. (1998) Parental socialization of emotion. *Psychological Inquiry*, 9: 241–273.

Ekman, P., and Friesen, W.V. (1976) *Pictures of Facial Affect*. Palo Alto, CA: Consulting Psychologists Press.

Elfenbein, H.A., and Ambady, N. (2002) On the universality and cultural specificity of emotion recognition: A meta-analysis. *Psychological Bulletin*, 128: 203–235.

Ellis, A.J., Beevers, C.G., and Wells, T.T. (2009) Emotional dysregulation in dysphoria: Support for emotion context insensitivity in response to performance-based feedback. *Journal of Behavior Therapy and Experimental Psychiatry*, 40: 443–454.

Ely, R., and Gleason, J.B. (1995) Socialization across contexts. In P. Fletcher and B. MacWhinney (eds) *Handbook of Child Language* (pp. 251–270). Oxford: Blackwell.

Emerich, D.M., Creaghead, N.A., Grether, S.M., Murray, D., and Grasha, C. (2003) The comprehension of humorous materials by adolescents with high-functioning autism and Asperger's syndrome. *Journal of Autism and Developmental Disorders*, 33: 253–257.

Everett, D. (2008) *Don't Sleep, There Are Snakes*. London: Profile Books.

Eysenck, H.J. (1967) *The Biological Basis of Personality*. Springfield, IL: Charles C. Thomas.

Fagot, B.I. (1997) Attachment, parenting, and peer interactions of toddler children. *Developmental Psychology*, 33: 489–499.

Feldman, R., Greenbaum, C.W., Mayes, L.C., and Erlich, S.H. (1997) Change in mother–infant interactive behavior: Relations to change in the mother, the infant, and the social context. *Infant Behavior and Development*, 20: 151–163.

Feldman-Barrett, L. (2004) Feelings or words? Understanding the content in self-report ratings of emotional experience. *Journal of Personality and Social Psychology*, 87: 266–281.

Feldman-Barrett, L., Gross, J., Christensen, T., and Benvenuto, M. (2001) Emotion differentiation and regulation. *Cognition and Emotion*, 15: 713–724.

Fernald, A. (1992) Meaningful melodies in mothers' speech to infants. In H. Papoušek, U. Jürgens and M. Papoušek (eds) *Nonverbal Vocal Communication: Comparative and Developmental Approaches* (pp. 262–282). Cambridge: Cambridge University Press.

Fernald, A., and Kuhl, P.K. (1987) Acoustic determinants of infant preference for motherese speech. *Infant Behavior and Development*, 10: 279–293.

Fernald, A., Taeschmer, T., Dunn, J., Papoušek, M., Boysson-Bardies, B., and Fukui, I. (1989) A cross-language study of prosodic modifications in mothers' and fathers' speech to preverbal infants. *Journal of Child Language*, 16: 477–501.

Fernandez-Dols, J.M., and Ruiz-Belda, M.A. (1995) Are smiles a sign of happiness? Gold medal winners in the Olympic Games. *Journal of Personality and Social Psychology*, 69: 1113–1119.

Ferrier, L.J. (1978) Some observations of error in context. In N. Waterson and C. Snow (eds) *The Development of Communication* (pp. 301–309). Chichester: Wiley.

Field, T., Healy, B., Goldstein, S., and Guthertz, M. (1990) Behavior state matching and synchrony in mother–infant interactions of nondepressed versus 'depressed' dyads. *Developmental Psychology*, 26: 7–14.

Fogel, A., de Koeyer, I., and Bellagamba, H.B. (2002) The dialogical self in the first two years of life: Embarking on a journey of discovery. *Theory and Psychology*, 12 (2): 191–205.

Fortanet, I. (2004) The use of 'we' in university lectures: Reference and function. *English for Specific Purposes*, 23: 45–66.

Frankel, K.A., and Harmon, R.J. (1996) Depressed mothers: They don't always look as bad as they feel. *Journal of the American Academy of Child and Adolescent Psychiatry*, 35: 289–298.

Fredrickson, B.L. (1998) Cultivated emotions: Parental socialization of positive emotions and self-conscious emotions. *Psychological Inquiry*, 9: 279–281.

Furnham, A., and Petrides, K.V. (2003) Trait emotional intelligence and happiness. *Social Behavior and Personality*, 31: 815–823.

Gao, X., and Maurer, D. (2010) A happy story: Developmental changes in children's sensitivity to facial expressions of varying intensities. *Journal of Experimental Child Psychology*, 107: 67–86.

Gardner, H. (1983) *Multiple Intelligences*. New York: Basic Books.

Geangu, E., Benga, O., Stahl, D., and Striano, T. (2010) Contagious crying beyond the first days of life. *Infant Behavior and Development*, 33: 279–288.

George, J.M. (2000) Emotions and leadership: The role of emotional intelligence. *Human Relations*, 53: 1027–1055.

Gerits, L., Derksen, J.J., Verbruggen, A.B., and Katzko, M. (2005) Emotional intelligence profiles of nurses caring for people with severe behaviour problems. *Personality and Individual Differences*, 38: 33–43.

Gleason, J.B. (1975) Fathers and other strangers: Men's speech to young children. In D. Dato (ed.) *Developmental Psycholinguistics: Theory and Application, Georgetown University Roundtable on Language and Linguistics* (pp. 289–297). Washington, DC: Georgetown University Press.

Goleman, D. (1995) *Emotional Intelligence: Why It Can Matter More than IQ*. New York: Bantam.

Gottman, J., and Declaire, J. (1997) *The Heart of Parenting: Raising an Emotionally Intelligent Child*. New York: Simon & Schuster.

Green, G.M. (1989) *Pragmatics and Natural Language Understanding*. Hillsdale, NJ: Lawrence Erlbaum Associates.

Green, J., and Goldwyn, R. (2002) Annotation: Attachment disorganisation and psychopathology. New findings in attachment research and their potential implications for developmental psychopathology in childhood. *Journal of Child Psychology and Psychiatry*, 43: 835–846.

Greenberg, M.T., Kusche, C.A., Cook, E.T., and Quamma, J.P. (1995) Promoting emotional competence in school aged children: The effects of the PATHS curriculum. *Development and Psychopathology*, 7: 117–136.

Grolnick, W., Kurowski, C., McMenamy, J., Rivkin, I., and Bridges, L. (1998) Mothers' strategies for regulating their toddlers' distress. *Infant Behavior and Development*, 21: 437–450.

Gross, J.J., and Levenson, R.W. (1997) Hiding feelings: The acute effects of inhibiting negative and positive emotion. *Journal of Abnormal Psychology*, 106: 95–103.

Gross, J.J., and Thompson, R.A. (2007) Emotion regulation: Conceptual foundations. In J.J. Gross (ed.) *Handbook of Emotion Regulation* (pp. 3–24). New York: Guilford.

Gutstein, S.E., and Whitney, T. (2002) Asperger syndrome and the development of social competence. *Focus on Autism and Other Developmental Disabilities*, 17: 161–171.

Haidt, J., and Keltner, D. (1999) Culture and facial expression: Open ended methods find more expressions and a gradient of recognition. *Cognition and Emotion*, 13: 225–266.

Hawk, S.T., Kleef, G.A. van, Fischer, A.H., and Schalk, J. van der (2009) Worth a thousand words: Absolute and relative decodability of non-linguistic affect vocalizations. *Emotion*, 9: 293–305.

Hoffman, M.L. (1981) Perspectives on the difference between understanding people and understanding things: the role of affect. In J.H. Flavell and L. Ross (eds) *Social Cognitive Development* (pp. 67–81). Cambridge: Cambridge University Press.

Hopper, R., Sims, A.L., and Alberts, J.K. (1983) Teasing as Daddy's classroom: A preliminary conversational analysis. *First Language*, 4: 147–148.

Hornik, R., Risenhoover, N., and Gunnar, M. (1987) The effects of maternal positive, neutral, and negative affective communications on infant responses to new toys. *Child Development*, 58: 937–944.

Hunt, N., and Evans, D. (2004) Predicting traumatic stress using emotional intelligence. *Behaviour Research and Therapy*, 42: 791–798.

Hunt, N., and Robbins, I. (1998) Telling stories of the war: Ageing veterans coping with their memories through narrative. *Oral History*, 26: 57–64.

Isaacowitz, D.M., Loeckenhoff, C.E., Lane, R.D., Wright, R., Sechrest, L., Riedel, R., and Costa, P.T. (2007) Age differences in recognition of emotion in lexical stimuli and facial expressions. *Psychology and Aging*, 22: 147–159.

Isabella, R.A., Belsky, J., and von Eye, A. (1989) Origins of infant–mother attachment: An examination of interactional synchrony during the infant's first year. *Developmental Psychology*, 25 (1): 12–21.

Izard, C.E., and Ackerman, B.P. (2000) Motivational, organizational, and regulatory functions of discrete emotions. In M. Lewis and J.M. Haviland-Jones (eds) *Handbook of Emotions*, 2nd edn (pp. 253–264). New York: Guilford.

Izard, C.E., Hembree, E., Dougherty, L.M., and Spizzirri, C.C. (1983) Changes in facial expressions of 2–19 months old infants following acute pain. *Developmental Psychology*, 19: 418–426.

Jaffe, J., Beebe, B., Feldstein, S., Crown, C.L., and Jasnow, M.D. (2001) Rhythms of dialogue in infancy: Coordinated timing in development. *Monographs of the Society for Research in Child Development*, 66 (2): i–viii, 1–132.

Jahromi, L.B., and Stifter, C.A. (2007) Individual differences in the contribution of maternal soothing to infant distress reduction. *Infancy*, 11: 255–269.

Jahromi, L.B., Putnam, S.P., and Stifter, C.A. (2004) Maternal regulation of infant reactivity from 2 to 6 months. *Developmental Psychology*, 4: 477–487.

Jenkins, R., Rose, J., and Lovell, C. (1997) Psychological well-being of staff working with people who have challenging behaviour. *Journal of Intellectual Disability Research*, 41: 502–511.

Jones, J.C., Payne, R.L., and Flick, J.T. (1987) Some determinants of stress in psychiatric nurses. *International Journal of Nursing Studies*, 24: 129–144.

Joseph, D.L., and Newman, D.A. (2010) Emotional intelligence: An integrative meta-analysis and cascading model. *Journal of Applied Psychology*, 95: 54–78.

Kamio, A. (2001) English generic we, you, and they: An analysis in terms of territory of information. *Journal of Pragmatics*, 33: 1111–1124.

Kappas, H. (1967) A developmental analysis of children's responses to humour. *The Library Quarterly*, 37: 67–77.

Kasari, C., and Rotheram-Fuller, E. (2005) Current trends in psychological research on children with high-functioning autism and Asperger disorder: Mental retardation and developmental disorders. *Current Opinion in Psychiatry*, 18: 497–501.

Kaye, K. (1982) *The Mental and Social Life of Babies*. Brighton: Harvester.

Keltner, D., Young, R.C., Heerey, E.A., Oeming, C., and Monarch, N.D. (1998) Teasing in hierarchical and intimate relations. *Journal of Personality and Social Psychology*, 75: 1231–1247.

Keltner, D., Capps, L., Kring, A.M., Young, R.C., and Heerey, E. (2001) Just teasing: A conceptual analysis and empirical review. *Psychological Bulletin*, 127: 228–248.

Kendler, K.S., Neale, M.C., Kessler, R.C., Heath, A.C., and Eaves, L.J. (1992) Childhood parental loss and adult psychopathology in women. *Archives of General Psychiatry*, 49: 109–116.

Kennedy-Moore, E., and Watson, J.C. (1999) *Expressing Emotion: Myths, Realities and Therapeutic Strategies*. New York: Guilford.

Khouzam, H.R., El-Gabalawi, F., Pirwani, N., and Priest, F. (2004) Asperger's disorder: A review of its diagnosis and treatment. *Comprehensive Psychiatry*, 45 (3): 184–191.

Kitamura, C., and Burnham, D. (2003) Pitch and communicative intent in mother's speech: Adjustments for age and sex in the first year. *Infancy*, 4: 85–110.

Knafo, A., Zahn-Waxler, C., Davidov, M., Van Hulle, C., Robinson, J-A., and Rhee, S.H. (2009) Empathy in early childhood: Genetic, environmental, and affective contributions. *Annals of the New York Academy of Sciences*, 1167: 103–114.

Kochanska, G. (2001) Emotional development in children with different attachment histories: The first three years. *Child Development*, 72: 474–490.

Kochanska, G., and Aksan, N. (1995) Mother–child mutually positive affect, the quality of child compliance to requests and prohibitions, and maternal control as correlates of early internalization. *Child Development*, 66: 236–254.

Kromelow, S., Harding, C., and Touris, M. (1990) The role of the father in the development of stranger sociability during the second year. *American Journal of Orthopsychiatry*, 60: 521–530.

Kübler-Ross, E. (1969) *On Death and Dying*. New York: Scribner.

Kyratzis, A., and Guo, J. (1996) 'Separate worlds for girls and boys'? Views from U.S. and Chinese mixed-sex friendship groups. In D. Slobin, J. Gerhardt, A. Kyratzis and J. Guo (eds) *Social Interaction, Social Context, and Language* (pp. 555–575). Mahwah, NJ: Lawrence Erlbaum Associates.

Laakso, A., and Smith, L.B. (2004) Pronouns predict verb meanings in child-directed speech. In K. Forbus, D. Gentner and T. Regier (eds) *Proceedings of the 26th Annual Meeting of the Cognitive Science Society* (pp. 767–772). Mahwah, NJ: Lawrence Erlbaum Associates.

Labrell, F. (1994) Atypical interaction behavior between fathers and toddlers: Teasing. *Early Development and Parenting*, 3: 125–130.

Lamb, M.E., Frodi, A.M., Hwang, C-P., Frodi, M., and Steinberg, J. (1982) Mother- and father-infant interaction involving play and holding in traditional and nontraditional Swedish families. *Developmental Psychology*, 18: 215–221.

Lampert, M. (1996) Studying gender differences in the conversational humor of adults and children. In D. Slobin, J. Gerhardt, A. Kyratzis and J. Guo (eds) *Social Interaction, Social Context, and Language* (pp. 579–596). Mahwah, NJ: Lawrence Erlbaum Associates.

Lavelli, M., and Fogel, A. (2005) Developmental changes in the relationship between the infant's attention and emotion during early face-to-face communication: The 2-month transition. *Developmental Psychology*, 41 (1): 265–280.

Leary, M.R., Springer, G., Negel, L., Ansell, E., and Evans, K. (1998) The causes, phenomenology, and consequences of hurt feelings. *Journal of Personality and Social Psychology*, 74: 1225–1237.

Leinonen, L., Hiltunen, T., Linnankoski, I., and Laakso, M-L. (1997) Expression of emotional motivational connotations with a one-word utterance. *Journal of Acoustical Society of America*, 102: 1853–1863.

Lewis, M. (1995) Aspects of self: From systems to ideas. In P. Rochat (ed.) *The Self in Early Infancy: Theory and Research* (pp. 95–115). Amsterdam: Elsevier.

Lewis, M. (2001) Origins of the self-conscious child. In R. Crozier and L.E. Alden (eds) *International Handbook of Social Anxiety: Concepts, Research, and Interventions Relating to Self and Shyness* (pp. 101–118). Chichester: Wiley.

Lewis, M., and Feiring, C. (1991) Attachment as personal characteristic or a measure of the environment. In J.L. Gewirtz and W.M. Kurtines (eds) *Intersections with Attachment* (pp. 3–21). Hillside, NJ: Lawrence Erlbaum Associates.

Lewis, M., and Ramsey, D. (2004) Development of self-recognition, personal pronoun use, and pretend play during the 2nd year. *Child Development*, 75: 1821–1831.

Lewis, M.D. (2000) Emotional self-organization at three time scales. In M.D. Lewis and I. Granic (eds) *Emotion, Development, and Self-organization: Dynamic Systems Approaches to Emotional Development* (pp. 37–69). New York: Cambridge University Press.

Locke, E.A. (2005) Why emotional intelligence is an invalid concept. *Journal of Organizational Behavior*, 26: 425–431.

Lopes, P.N., Salovey, P., Cote, S., and Beers, M. (2005) Emotion regulation abilities and the quality of social interaction. *Emotion*, 5: 113–118.

McGrath, A., Reid, N., and Boose, J. (2003) Occupational stress in nursing. *International Journal of Nursing Studies*, 26: 343–358.

Malatesta, C.Z. (1990) The role of emotion in the organization of personality. In R.A. Thompson (ed.) *Nebraska Symposium on Motivation*: vol. 36, *Socioemotional Development* (pp. 1–56). Lincoln, NE: University of Nebraska Press.

Malatesta, C.Z., and Haviland, J.M. (1982) Learning display rules: The socialization of emotion expression in infancy. *Child Development*, 53: 991–1003.

Maltz, D., and Borker, R. (1982) A cultural approach to male–female miscommunication. In J.J. Gumpertz (ed.) *Language and Social Identity* (pp. 195–216). Cambridge: Cambridge University Press.

Manassis, K., Bradley, S., Goldberg, S., Hood, J., and Swinson, R.P. (1994) Attachment in mothers with anxiety disorders and their children. *Journal of the American Academy of Child and Adolescent Psychiatry*, 33: 1106–1113.

Martins, A., Ramalho, N., and Morin, E. (2010) A comprehensive meta-analysis of the relationship between emotional intelligence and health. *Personality and Individual Differences*, 49: 554–564.

Masur, E.F. (1983) Gestural development, dual-directional signaling, and the transition to words. *Journal of Psycholinguistic Research*, 12: 93–109.

Matsumoto, D., LeRoux, J., and Wilson-Cohn, C. (2000) A new test to measure emotion recognition ability: Matsumoto and Ekman's Japanese and Caucasian Brief Affect Recognition Test (JACBART). *Journal of Nonverbal Behavior*, 24: 179–209.

Matthews, G., Zeidner, M., and Roberts, R.D. (2002) *Emotional Intelligence: Science and Myth*. Cambridge, MA: MIT Press.

Mavroveli, S., Petrides, K.V., Shove, C., and Whitehead, A. (2008) Investigation of the construct of trait emotional intelligence in children. *European Child and Adolescent Psychiatry*, 17: 516–526.

Mayer, J.D., and Salovey, P. (1997) What is emotional intelligence? In P. Salovey and D. Sluyter (eds) *Emotional Development and Emotional Intelligence: Implications for Educators* (pp. 3–31). New York: Basic Books.

Mayer, J.D., Caruso, D.R., and Salovey, P. (1999) Emotional intelligence meets traditional standards for emotional intelligence. *Intelligence*, 27: 267–298.

Mayer, J.D., Caruso, D.R., and Salovey, P. (2000) Selecting a measure of emotional intelligence: The case of ability scales. In R. Bar-On and J.D.A.

Parker (eds) *The Handbook of Emotional Intelligence* (pp. 320–342). San Francisco, CA: Jossey-Bass.

Mayer, J.D., Salovey, P., Caruso, D.R., and Sitarenios, G. (2001) Emotional intelligence as a standard intelligence. *Emotion*, 1: 232–242.

Mayer, J.D., Salovey, P., and Caruso, D.R. (eds) (2002) *Mayer-Salovey-Caruso Emotional Intelligence Test (MSCEIT), Version 2.0*. Toronto: Multi-Health Systems.

Mayer, J.D., Salovey, P., Caruso, D.R., and Sitarenios, G. (2003) Measuring emotional intelligence with the MSCEIT V2.0. *Emotion*, 3: 97–105.

Mayer, J.D., Roberts, R.D., and Barsade, S.G. (2008) Human abilities: Emotional intelligence. *Annual Review of Psychology*, 59: 507–536.

Messinger, D., and Fogel, A. (2007) The interactive development of social smiling. In R.V. Kail (ed.) *Advances in Child Development and Behavior* (pp. 327–366). Amsterdam: Elsevier.

Messinger, D., Fogel, A., and Dickson, K.L. (1997) A dynamic systems approach to infant facial action. In J.A. Russell and F.M. Dols (eds) *The Psychology of Facial Expression* (pp. 205–226). New York: Cambridge University Press.

Mikolajczak, M., Nelis, D., Hansenne, M., and Quoidbach, J. (2008) If you can regulate sadness, you can probably regulate shame: Associations between trait emotional intelligence, emotion regulation and coping efficiency across discrete emotions. *Personality and Individual Differences*, 44: 1356–1368.

Miller, P. (1986) Teasing as language socialization and verbal play in a white working-class community. In B.B. Schieffelin and E. Ochs (eds) *Language Socialization across Cultures* (pp. 199–212). New York: Cambridge University Press.

Mischel, W., Shoda, Y., and Peake, P.K. (1988) The nature of adolescent competencies predicted by preschool delay of gratification. *Journal of Personality and Social Psychology*, 54: 687–696.

Montgomery, J.M., McCrimmon, A.W., Schwean, V.L., and Saklofske, D.H. (2010) Emotional intelligence in Asperger syndrome: Implications of dissonance between intellect and affect. *Education and Training in Autism and Developmental Disabilities*, 45: 566–582.

Mooney, A., Creeser, R., and Blatchford, P. (1991) Children's views on teasing and fighting in junior schools. *Educational Research*, 33: 103–112.

Morton, J.B., and Trehub, S.E. (2001) Children's understanding of emotion in speech. *Child Development*, 72: 834–843.

Murphy, K.R. (2006) Four conclusions about emotional intelligence. In K.R. Murphy (ed.) *A Critique of Emotional Intelligence* (pp. 345–354). Mahwah, NJ: Lawrence Erlbaum Associates.

Murray, L. (1992) The impact of postnatal depression on infant development. *Journal of Child Psychology and Psychiatry*, 33: 543–561.

Murray, L., Kempton, C., Woolgar, M., and Hooper, R. (1993) Depressed mothers' speech to their infants and its relationship to infant gender and cognitive development. *Journal of Child Psychology and Psychiatry*, 34: 1083–1101.

Nelson, K.E. (1975) The nominal shift in semantic-syntactic development. *Cognitive Psychology*, 7: 461–479.

Newport, E.L., Gleitman, H., and Gleitman, L.R. (1977) Mother I'd rather do it myself: Some effects and non-effects of maternal speech style. In C.E. Snow and C.A. Ferguson (eds) *Talking to Children: Language Input and Acquisition* (pp. 109–149). Cambridge: Cambridge University Press.

Ortony, A., Turner, T.J., and Larson-Shapiro, N. (1985) Cultural and instructional influences on figurative language comprehension by inner city children. *Research in the Teaching of English*, 19: 25–36.

Papoušek, H., and Papoušek, M. (2002) Intuitive parenting. In M.H. Bornstein (ed.) *Handbook of Parenting*: vol. 2, *Biology and Ecology of Parenting*, 2nd edn (pp. 183–203). Mahwah, NJ: Lawrence Erlbaum Associates.

Papoušek, I., Freudenthaler, H.H., and Schulter, G. (2008) The interplay of perceiving and regulating emotions in becoming infected with positive and negative moods. *Personality and Individual Differences*, 45: 463–467.

Papoušek, M. (1992) Early ontogeny of vocal communication in parent–infant interactions. In H. Papoušek, U. Jürgens and M. Papoušek (eds) *Nonverbal Vocal Communication: Comparative and Developmental Approaches* (pp. 230–261). Cambridge: Cambridge University Press.

Patel, A.D. (2003) A new approach to the cognitive neuroscience of melody. In I. Peretz and R. Zatorre (eds) *The Cognitive Neuroscience of Music* (pp. 325–345). Oxford: Oxford University Press.

Paulos, J.A. (1980) *Mathematics and Humor*. Chicago, IL: University of Chicago Press.

Pecheux, M.G., and Labrell, F. (1994) Parent–infant interactions and early cognitive development. In A. Vyt, H. Bloch and M. Bornstein (eds) *Early Child Development in the French Tradition* (pp. 255–267). Hillsdale, NJ: Lawrence Erlbaum Associates.

Pell, M.D. (2001) Influence of emotion and focus on prosody in matched statements and questions. *Journal of the Acoustical Society of America*, 109: 1668–1680.

Petrides, K.V., and Furnham, A. (2003) Trait emotional intelligence: Behavioural validation in two studies of emotion recognition and reactivity to mood induction. *European Journal of Personality*, 17: 39–57.

Petrides, K.V., and Sevdalis, N. (2010) Emotional intelligence and nursing: Comment on Bulmer-Smith, Profetto-McGrath, and Cummings (2009). *International Journal of Nursing Studies*, 47: 526–528.

Petrides, K.V., Furnham, A., and Mavroveli, S. (2007) Trait emotional intelligence: Moving forward in the field of EI. In G. Matthews, M. Zeidner and R. Roberts (eds) *The Science of Emotional Intelligence: Knowns and Unknowns* (pp. 151–166). Oxford: Oxford University Press.

Pinderhughes, E., and Zigler, E. (1985) Cognitive and motivational determinants of children's humor responses. *Journal of Research in Personality*, 19: 185–196.

Pruett, K.D. (1998) Role of the father. *Pediatrics*, 102: 1253–1261.

Putnam, S.P., Spritz, B.L., and Stifter, C.A. (2002) Mother–child coregulation during delay of gratification at 30 months. *Infancy*, 3: 209–225.

Reddy, V. (1991) Playing with others' expectations: Teasing and mucking about in the first year. In A. Whiten (ed.) *Natural Theories of Mind: Evolution, Development, and Stimulation of Everyday Mind Reading* (pp. 143–158). Oxford: Blackwell.

Reissland, N. (1990) Parental frameworks of pleasure and pride. *Infant Behavior and Development*, 13: 249–256.

Reissland, N. (1994) The socialization of pride in young children. *International Journal of Behavioral Development*, 17: 541–552.

Reissland, N. (1995) How angels become real. *Common Knowledge*, 4: 1–6.

Reissland, N. (1998) The pitch of 'real' and 'rhetorical' questions directed by a father to his daughter: A longitudinal case study. *Infant Behavior and Development*, 21: 793–798.

Reissland, N., and Burt, M. (2010) Bi-directional effects of depressed mood in the postnatal period on mother– infant nonverbal engagement with picture books. *Infant Behavior and Development*, 33: 613–618.

Reissland, N., and Shepherd, J. (2002) Gaze direction and maternal pitch in surprise-eliciting situations. *Infant Behavior and Development*, 24: 408–417.

Reissland, N., and Shepherd, J. (2006) The effect of maternal depressed mood on infant emotional reaction. *Infant Mental Health Journal*, 27: 173–187.

Reissland, N., and Snow, D. (1996) Maternal pitch height in ordinary and play situations. *Journal of Child Language*, 23: 1–10.

Reissland, N., Shepherd, J., and Stephenson, T. (1999) Maternal verbal interaction in different situations with infants born prematurely or at term. *Infant and Child Development*, 8: 39–48.

Reissland, N., Shepherd, J., and Cowie, L. (2002) The melody of surprise: Maternal surprise vocalizations during play with her infant. *Infant and Child Development*, 11: 271–278.

Reissland, N., Shepherd, J., and Herrera, E. (2003) The pitch of maternal voice: A comparison of mothers suffering from depressed mood and non-depressed mothers reading books to their infants. *Journal of Child Psychology and Psychiatry*, 44: 255–261.

Ruch, W., and Ekman, P. (2001) The expressive pattern of laughter. In A. Kaszniak (ed.) *Emotion, Qualia and Consciousness* (pp. 426–443). Tokyo: World Scientific Publisher.

Russell, J.A., Bachorowski, J.A., and Fernández-Dols, J.-M. (2003) Facial and vocal expressions of emotion. *Annual Review of Psychology*, 54: 329–349.

Ryan, D., and Quayle, E. (1999) Stress in psychiatric nursing: Fact or fiction? *Nursing Standard*, 14 (8): 32–35.

Saarni, C. (1999) *The Development of Emotional Competence.* New York: Guilford.

Saarni, C. (2001) The continuity dilemma in emotional competence. *Psychological Inquiry*, 12: 94–96.

Saklofske, D.H., Austin, E.J., and Minski, P.S. (2003) Factor structure and validity of a trait emotional intelligence measure. *Personality and Individual Differences*, 34: 707–721.

Salovey, P., and Grewal, D. (2005) The science of emotional intelligence. *Current Directions in Psychological Science*, 14: 281–285.

Salovey, P., and Mayer, J.D. (1990) Emotional intelligence. *Imagination, Cognition and Personality*, 9: 185–211.

Salovey, P., and Sluyter, D. (eds) (1997) *Emotional Development and Emotional Intelligence: Implications for Educators.* New York: Basic Books.

Salovey, P., Woolery, A., and Mayer, J.D. (2001) Emotional intelligence: Conceptualization and measurement. In G.J.O. Fletcher and M.S. Clark (eds) *Blackwell Handbook of Social Psychology: Interpersonal Processes* (pp. 279–307). Malden, MA: Blackwell.

Samson, A.C., and Hegenloh, M. (2010) Stimulus characteristics affect humor processing in individuals with Asperger syndrome. *Journal of Autism and Developmental Disorders*, 40: 438–447.

Sarid, O., Berger, R., and Segal-Engelchin, D. (2010) The impact of cognitive behavioral interventions on SOC, perceived stress and mood states of nurses. *Procedia – Social and Behavioral Sciences*, 2 (2): 928–932.

Scheier, M.F., Carver, C.S., and Bridges, M.W. (1994) Distinguishing optimism from neuroticism (and trait anxiety, self-mastery, and self-esteem): A re-evaluation of the Life Orientation Test. *Journal of Personality and Social Psychology*, 67: 1063–1078.

Scheier, M.F., Carver, C.S., and Bridges, M.W. (2001) Optimism, pessimism, and psychological well-being. In E.C. Chang (ed.) *Optimism and Pessimism: Implications for Theory, Research, and Practice* (pp. 189–216). Washington, DC: American Psychological Association.

Scherer, K.R. (2009) The dynamic architecture of emotion: Evidence for the component process model. *Cognition and Emotion*, 23: 1307–1351.

Scherer, K.R., and Ellgring, H. (2007) Are facial expressions of emotion produced by categorical affect programs or dynamically driven by appraisal? *Emotion*, 7: 113–130.

Scherer, K.R., Banse, R., Wallbott, H.G., and Goldbeck, T. (1991) Vocal cues in emotion encoding and decoding. *Motivation and Emotion*, 15: 123–148.

Schlegloff, E.A. (1979) Identification and recognition in telephone conversation openings. In G. Psathas (ed.) *Everyday Language: Studies in Ethnomethodology* (pp. 23–78). New York: Irvington.

Scholmerich, A., Fracasso, M., Lamb, M., and Broberg, A. (1995) Interactional harmony at 7 and 10 months of age predicts security of attachment as measured by Q-sort ratings. *Social Development*, 4: 62–74.

Schutte, N.S., Malouff, J.M., Bobik, C., Conston, T., Greeson, C., Jedlicka,

C. et al. (2001) Emotional intelligence and interpersonal relations. *Journal of Social Psychology*, 141: 523–536.

Schutte, N.S., Malouff, J.M., Simunek, M., Hollander, S., and McKenley, J. (2002) Characteristic emotional intelligence and emotional well-being. *Cognition and Emotion*, 16: 769–786.

Schutte, N.S., Malouff, J.M., Thorsteinsson, E.B., Bhullar, N., and Rooke, S.E. (2007) A meta-analytic investigation of the relationship between emotional intelligence and health. *Personality and Individual Differences*, 42: 921–933.

Sevdalis, N., Petrides, K.V., and Harvey, N. (2007) Trait emotional intelligence and decision-related emotions. *Personality and Individual Differences*, 42: 1347–1358.

Shapiro, J.P., Baumeister, R.F., and Kessler, J.W. (1991) A three component model of children's teasing: Aggression, humor, and ambiguity. *Journal of Social and Clinical Psychology*, 10: 459–472.

Sharkey, W.F. (1992) Uses of and responses to intentional embarrassment. *Communication Studies*, 43: 257–275.

Sherrod, K.B., Friedman, S., Crawley, S., Drake, D., and Devieux, J. (1977) Maternal language to prelinguistic infants: Syntactic aspects. *Child Development*, 48: 1662–1665.

Siegel, G.M., Cooper, M., Morgan, J.L., and Brenneise-Sarshad, R. (1990) Imitation of intonation by infants. *Journal of Speech and Hearing Research*, 33: 9–15.

Slaski, M., and Cartwright, S. (2002) Health, performance and emotional intelligence: An exploratory study of retail managers. *Stress and Health*, 18: 63–68.

Snow, C.E. (1977) The development of conversation between mothers and babies. *Journal of Child Language*, 4: 1–22.

Snow, C.E., and Goldfield, B.A. (1983) Turn the page please: Situation specific language acquisition. *Journal of Child Language*, 10: 551–569.

Snow, C.E., Arlman-Rupp, A., Hassing, Y., Jobse, J., Joosten, J., and Vorster, J. (1976) Mothers' speech in three social classes. *Journal of Psycholinguistic Research*, 5: 1–20.

Soussignan, R. (2002) Duchenne smile, emotional experience, and autonomic reactivity: A test of the facial feedback hypothesis. *Emotion*, 2: 52–74.

Southam-Gerow, M.A., and Kendall, P.C. (2002) Emotion regulation and understanding: Implications for child psychopathology and therapy. *Clinical Psychology Review*, 22: 189–222.

Sroufe, L.A. (1995) The development of joy: A prototype for the study of emotion. In L.A. Sroufe, *Emotional Development: The Organization of Emotional Life in the Early Years* (pp. 77–100). Cambridge : Cambridge University Press.

Sroufe, L.A. (1997) *Emotional Development*. New York: Cambridge University Press.

Sroufe, L.A., and Wunsch, J.P. (1972) The development of laughter in the first year of life. *Child Development*, 43: 1326–1344.

Stern, D.N. (1985) *The Interpersonal World of the Infant: A View from Psychoanalysis and Developmental Psychology.* New York: Basic Books.

Stern, D.N., Spieker, S., and MacKain, K. (1982) Intonation contours in maternal speech to prelinguistic children. *Developmental Psychology*, 18 (5): 727–735.

Sullivan, J.W., and Horowitz, F.D. (1983) Infant intermodal perception and maternal multimodal stimulation: Implications for language development. In L.P. Lipsitt and C. Rovee-Collier (eds) *Advances in Infancy Research*, vol. 2 (pp. 183–239). Norwood, NJ: Ablex.

Szameitat, D.P., Alter, K., Szameitat, A.J., Wildgruber, D., Sterr, A., and Darwin, C.J. (2009) Acoustic profiles of distinct emotional expressions in laughter. *Journal of the Acoustical Society of America*, 126 (1): 354–366.

Tomasello, M. (1992) *First Verbs.* Cambridge: Cambridge University Press.

Tracy, J.L., and Robins, R.W. (2008) The automaticity of emotion recognition. *Emotion*, 8: 81–95.

Trehub, S.E., Unyk, A.M., Kamenetsky, S.B., Hill, D.S., Trainor, L.J., Henderson, J.L., and Saraza, M. (1997) Mothers' and fathers' singing to infants. *Developmental Psychology*, 33: 500–507.

Trevarthen, C. (2001) Intrinsic motives for companionship in understanding: Their origin, development, and significance for infant mental health. *Infant Mental Health Journal*, 22 (1–2): 95–131.

Trevarthen, C., and Hubley, P. (1978) Secondary intersubjectivity: Confidence, confiding and acts of meaning in the first year. In A. Lock (ed.) *Action, Gesture and Symbol: The Emergence of Language* (pp. 183–230). London: Academic Press.

Tronick, E.Z. (1989) Emotions and emotional communication in infants. *American Psychologist*, 44 (2). 112–119.

van Rijn, S., Schothorst, P., van 't Wout, M., Sprong, M., Ziermans, T., van Engeland, H. et al. (2011) Affective dysfunctions in adolescents at risk for psychosis: Emotion awareness and social functioning. *Psychiatry Research*, 187: 100–105.

Vicari, S., Reilly, J.S., Pasqualetti, P., Vizzotto, A., and Caltagirone, C. (2000) Recognition of facial expressions of emotions in school-age children: The intersection of perceptual and semantic categories. *Acta Paediatrica*, 89: 836–845.

Wang, Q. (2001) 'Did you have fun?': American and Chinese mother child conversations about shared emotional experiences. *Cognitive Development*, 16: 693–715.

Warm, T.R. (1997) The role of teasing in development and vice versa. *Journal of Developmental and Behavioural Pediatrics*, 18: 97–101.

Warren-Leubecker, A., and Bohannon III, J.N. (1984) Intonation patterns of child-directed speech: Mother–father differences. *Child Development*, 55: 1379–1385.

Waterson, N. (1978) Growth of complexity in phonological development. In N. Waterson and C. Snow (eds) *The Development of Communication* (pp. 415–442). Chichester: Wiley.

Watson, D. (2000) *Mood and Temperament*. New York: Guilford.

Widen, S.C., and Russell, J.A. (2003) A closer look at preschoolers' freely produced labels for facial expressions. *Developmental Psychology*, 39: 114–128.

Wing, L. (1981) Language, social, and cognitive impairments in autism and severe mental retardation. *Journal of Autism and Developmental Disorders*, 11: 31–44.

Winkielman, P., Berridge, K., and Wilbarger, J.L. (2005) Unconscious affective reactions to masked happy versus angry faces influence consumption behavior and judgements of value. *Personality and Social Psychology Bulletin*, 31: 121–135.

Yik, M.S.M., Meng, Z., and Russell, J.A. (1998) Brief report: Adults' freely produced emotion labels for babies' spontaneous facial expressions. *Cognition and Emotion*, 12: 723–730.

Zahn-Waxler, C., and Radke-Yarrow, M. (1990) The origins of empathic concern. *Motivation and Emotion*, 14: 107–130.

Zahn-Waxler, C., Cummings, E.M., Iannotti, R.J., and Radke-Yarrow, M. (1984) Young offspring of depressed parents: A population at risk for affective problems. *New Directions for Child and Adolescent Development*, 26: 81–105.

Zeidner, M., Matthews, G., Roberts, R.D., and McCann, C. (2003) Development of emotional intelligence: Towards a multi-level investment model. *Human Development*, 46: 69–96.

Zigler, E., Levine, J., and Gould, L. (1966) Cognitive processes in the development of children's appreciation of humor. *Child Development*, 37: 507–518.

Index